What Next, Doctor?

Dr ROBERT CLIFFORD

Illustrated by Nick Baker

SPHERE BOOKS LIMITED

A SPHERE BOOK

First published in Great Britain in 1979 by Pelham Books Ltd
Published by Sphere Books 1981
Reprinted 1985, 1986, 1987, 1988, 1991

ISBN 0 7221 2381 7

Printed and bound in Great Britain by
BPCC Hazell Books
Aylesbury, Bucks, England
Member of BPCC Ltd.

Sphere Books Ltd
A Division of
Macdonald & Co (Publishers) Ltd
165 Great Dover Street
London SE1 4YA

A member of Maxwell Macmillan Publishing Corporation

THE PATIENT WHO DEFIED DIAGNOSIS . . .

'Eh, Doctor,' said Sam, 'I'm having a bit of trouble with me . . .'

'I see. With your . . .'

'No. With me . . .'

'Not your . . . ?'

'Yes. Especially in the middle of the . . .'

'During the . . . ?'

'That's it. Give me terrible cramps in me . . .'

'Oh dear. Does it ever spread to your . . . ?'

'Yes. Gives me gyp, it does.'

'But you've never had it in your . . . ?'

'Not so far, no.'

'Well that's not so bad, I shouldn't worry, Sam, unless it spreads to your . . .'

'Eh, d'you think it might?'

Also by Robert Clifford in Sphere Books:

JUST HERE, DOCTOR
NOT THERE, DOCTOR
LOOK OUT, DOCTOR!
OH DEAR, DOCTOR!
SURELY NOT, DOCTOR!
THERE YOU ARE, DOCTOR!
ON HOLIDAY AGAIN DOCTOR?
YOU'RE STILL A DOCTOR, DOCTOR
THREE TIMES A DAY, DOCTOR?

Contents

Prologue

Life is a tragedy, for we are all born eventually to die.
We survive our tragedies by laughing at them.

*A friend once told me that when he was under the
influence of ether he dreamed he was turning over the
pages of a great book, in which he knew he would find,
on the last page, the meaning of life.*

*The pages of the book were alternately tragic and
comic, and he turned page after page, his excitement
growing, not only because he was approaching the
answer, but because he couldn't know, until he arrived,
on which side of the book the final page would be.
At last it came: the universe opened up to him in a
hundred words: and they were uproariously funny.*

*He came back to consciousness crying with laughter,
remembering everything. He opened his lips to speak.
It was then that the great and comic answer plunged
back out of his reach.*

Christopher Fry

I

Rude Awakening

I could hear a persistent knocking as I struggled to rouse myself from a deep sleep. My surroundings seemed strange, and in my half conscious state I couldn't work out where the knocking was coming from.

As I slowly surfaced I realised that I was in bed with Pam, that we were in an hotel in Cornwall, and that somebody was knocking at our bedroom door.

Then I remembered that Pam and I had been married the day before. We had motored through the night from Leatherhead in Surrey to the Carbis Bay Hotel at St Ives, Cornwall, arriving at three o'clock in the morning. We had ordered breakfast in bed for ten o'clock – our first breakfast together –

hoping the long lie-in would help recharge our batteries after the exhausting ordeal of our wedding and reception, followed by the slogging 300-mile drive down to Cornwall.

Having collected all these thoughts together, I was able to shout 'Come in!' to what had started as a tentative knocking and was now an exasperated hammering.

The door crashed open, and in walked an elderly, cross-faced, grey-haired lady, bearing a breakfast tray laden with coffee, boiled eggs, cornflakes and grapefruit.

'I've been hammering for hours!' she snapped. 'It's not good enough. I have had to walk up all these stairs – the lift isn't working. Fancy an old woman like me having to wait on young'uns like you. I've got arthritis, and the doctor says I shouldn't really be working at all.'

To prove her point, she limped across the room, and almost tipped the breakfast tray on our bed in transit.

'I don't know what young people are coming to nowadays,' she growled. 'Lying in bed till this time on a glorious day like this.'

We cringed self-consciously under the sheets.

The old woman grumpily put the tray down on a table at the foot of the bed. 'I hope it isn't going to be like this every morning,' she said as she stumped out. 'You want to get up and get out and get some fresh air.'

Pam and I lay in bed not talking, both very embarrassed. This was the first night we had ever shared a bed together, and to be attacked in it by a third party was something we hadn't bargained for.

We had looked forward to a long lie-in, and a leisurely breakfast. If we were not careful, this limping dragon was going to spoil it for us.

I got out of bed, collected the tray and put it down between us on the eiderdown.

'Come on, darling,' I said. 'Let's forget her and enjoy our first breakfast.'

We set out to make the best of it, but the coffee was cold, there was no sugar for the grapefruit, the eggs were hard-boiled, the toast was warped and snapped when we tried to butter it, there was hardly enough milk for the coffee, never mind the cornflakes, and after a few feeble attempts we gave up.

A breakfast as bad as this had not arrived by accident. Our chambermaid had deliberately made it inedible so that rather than face it in our room every morning, we would stagger down to breakfasts, however tired we were.

Pam had tears in her eyes. The first morning of our honeymoon should have been better than this. I put my arm round her. 'Never mind, darling,' I murmured. 'You've still got me.' (That's the kind of thing you can say only early on in a marriage.)

Then I remembered. 'Hang on,' I said, 'all is not lost.'

I rummaged in my case and came out with a long oblong box. This had been given to me by a patient, Simon Eggleton. Written on the box in bold letters were the words TO BE OPENED ON THE FIRST MORNING OF YOUR HONEYMOON.

We opened the box, and there was a huge magnum of champagne. Written on a card tied to it were the instructions –

THE ONLY POSSIBLE FIRST BREAKFAST FOR YOUR HONEYMOON, DOC AND MRS DOC. DON'T DILUTE IT WITH TOAST AND MARMALADE, JUST DRINK IT NEAT, AS DIRECTED

'We can't drink champagne for breakfast,' Pam said.

'Rubbish,' I replied. 'It's just the thing.'

I walked across to the washstand and rinsed out the tooth mugs. I popped the champagne cork, and we sat in bed, mugs in our hands, looking out across the bay and toasting each other as Mr and Mrs.

'I think, darling, that Simon must have been in collusion with the chambermaid', I said, 'But for her breakfast we could have forgotten his present. I'm afraid I can't promise that breakfasts in future will be quite up to this standard, but I will do my very best.'

Pam giggled. A couple of mugsful of champagne at this time

in the morning, on an empty stomach, was perhaps not the way to get a sensible answer.

*   *   *

Simon Eggleton was unique in that he was the only man I have ever treated for serious frostbite in the middle of a Somerset summer. He had been unloading boxes of frozen peas from a refrigeration van without wearing protective gloves. His hands, cold at first, soon became so frozen that he did not feel a thing. It was only a couple of hours afterwards, when they started to thaw out, that his troubles began.

When I was called to him he was actually screaming with pain and the top two joints of his fingers on both hands were a nasty bluish colour. His pain was so bad that I had to give him an injection of morphia and send him to Tadchester Hospital.

We thought he was going to lose his fingers. They were severely frostbitten. Their colour did not improve and he was in constant pain. Frostbite being uncommon in Somerset, we had to ring London for guidance on the management and outlook for his condition. He was three weeks in hospital under intensive treatment.

It was a long and prolonged battle. Even after discharge from hospital he had to attend the out-patients department for treatment for several further weeks. His fingers survived but he was left with some permanent loss of sensation in all his finger tips. This was quite a handicap. It meant that he was unable to assess heat and was always burning his fingers in hot water or on stoves and fires. He was unable to feel when a cigarette had burnt down to the skin level and had two permanent burns on his first and second fingers.

There was a long legal battle over his injury and he was eventually offered £25 compensation. I encouraged him to stick out for more, supporting him with some very firm medical letters, and with my support he finally settled for £500.

Simon Eggleton sent me a book token for £15 for all my help, and had come round to the wedding reception with the box that made our breakfast.

*   *   *

I had met Pam a year before while on holiday with my mother. At first she had thought my young-looking mother and I were husband and wife – but when I was affectionately bringing Pam round after having knocked her over on the squash court, she realised I was not an unfaithful husband but an ardent suitor.

We had become engaged at my teaching hospital's New Year Ball, and had married in her home town of Leatherhead. After our fortnight's honeymoon Pam would return with me to the Somerset coastal town of Tadchester and start married life in earnest as the young doctor's wife.

I had been in Tadchester for two years by the time of our marriage, and was the junior partner in a group of four doctors. Tadchester (population 6,500 stands on the estuary of the River Tad, in one of the most beautiful parts of the Somerset coast. It is a market town, with some fishing, some light industry, and a great deal of farming. Six miles north is Thudrock Colliery, half of whose work force lives in Tadchester.

The town is split in two by the River Tad, and further split by the large hill which dominates one side of the river. The other side of the river is flat pastureland, stretching off to marshes and the sea coast. You are not just a Tadchester resident – you are strictly Up-the-Hill or Down-the-Hill. It had important social distinctions: the population Down-the-Hill tended to be made up of Haves, the population of Up-the-Hill tended to be the Have-nots.

We were the only general practice in the town, and in addition to our general practice duties took care of the local hospital. There were four partners, each with a special interest at the hospital. Steve Maxwell, the senior partner, had a special interest in medicine. Henry Johnson, the second senior, was the surgeon. Jack Hart, the third partner, was the anaesthetist. I, as

13

the junior dogsbody, did most of the running around and was reckoned to be the expert in midwifery.

We practised from a central surgery Down-the-Hill, above which, before my marriage, I had a bachelor flat. There I fended for myself, living mainly on scrambled eggs and baked beans and suffering from a strange combination of malnutrition and indigestion.

*   *   *

Our wedding day had started disastrously. As the bridesmaids – Zara and Janice – entered the church, it was seen that their dresses were transparent. Both of them were unwittingly displaying most of their usually hidden physical charms to the congregation, bringing the colour back to the cheeks of all the male guests.

The day became almost a complete disaster when, as we were actually about to sign the register in the vestry, it was found that the vicar had omitted part of the wedding service. My best man, Eric Martin, was trying to draw everybody's attention to the fact that he still had not performed his one duty of handing over the wedding ring.

The wedding reception at the Bull Hotel, Leatherhead, passed as a blur. There were so many faces, so many congratulations, so many kisses that it was difficult to identify people individually. There were many of my friends from hospital days who I had not seen for some time, as well as the new friends I had made at Tadchester. There was a back-up of ancient aunts, uncles, nieces and cousins who had come from all over the British Isles, who only appeared at weddings and funerals, and tried to catch up in a few minutes with all the family happenings of the last few years.

With rugby friends from both Tadchester and London, and a free bar, the reception got steadily noisier. Zara and Janice in their revealing attire were surrounded by admirers and became so popular as the party became more inebriated that they retired to put on jumpers over their transparent wedding apparel.

This was like shutting the stable door after the horse had gone. Their uninhibited contours continued to make their points through their clinging jumpers. And the fact that they still looked as if they were naked from the waist down meant their jumpers had literally only halved their problem.

The wedding speeches eventually broke up the throng of the girls' admirers. The main speech was given by Mr Hogston, the father of Audrey Hogston, Pam's best friend almost from birth. He recounted Pam's life story from the Brownies onwards until she eventually met me. The Hogstons had been like a second father and mother to Pam and anybody marrying her had to pass their inspection. They were rugby enthusiasts and supported the Wasps, so the fact that I was a rugby player stood me in good stead.

Mr Hogston gave a very human, moving speech, with all the usual good wishes. He was followed by my Uncle Bertie, my mother's brother. Bertie was not on the speakers' list, but was always irrepressible on any social occasion. He was a great wit and should really have gone on the stage. As usual, with a few drinks on board, he got carried away and his stories and anecdotes became bluer and bluer. Eventually, my mother cut him short with a stage whisper 'Bertie! Behave yourself and *sit down*!'

The last speech was by Eric, my best man. He had to propose the toast of the bridesmaids. His was the shortest and most successful speech of all. He was half in his cups when he stood up and began, 'It is my duty to toast the bridesmaids . . .' He took one long, lecherous look at Zara (his bride-to-be, the chief and most uninhibited bridesmaid) and continued, 'I would much rather eat both of them untoasted', then sat down to a thunderous ovation.

Pam and I walked round together receiving our guests, talking to friends and relatives, having drinks. We cut the cake to boisterous applause, were photographed, and then at last the time came for us to go away and change. Returning in our going away clothes, somehow we struggled through confetti storms to reach my bedecked Morris Minor. Kisses, more kisses. Good byes, good byes, good byes. Then at last we were away. I stopped round the first corner to remove all the boots, saucepan lids, and bottles that were tied to the back of the car. Then off on our 300 mile drive to Cornwall.

We knew that we had a long and tedious drive ahead of us, most of it through the night, but we were full of beans. We had had a lovely wedding, and we knew that we had two uninterrupted weeks ahead of us. We also knew that whatever time we arrived, we could have a long lie-in and a lazy breakfast in bed the following morning.

2

Back to Work

I had always loved the St Ives area of Cornwall. When I was a medical student the hospital's rugby fifteen came to St Ives every Easter to play against the surrounding towns. We stayed in a different hotel every year, not because we were trying to find the best, but because one visit was the most any hotel would put up with. Next year there were always no vacancies.

In my last year as a medical student we had finally exhausted the St Ives hotels and booked in to the Carbis Bay Hotel, three miles out of the town. It was there that Pam and I had come to spend our honeymoon. I had taken some risk in choosing this area. When I was playing rugby I was young and fancy free and there could well be one or two young ladies who'd remember my amorous advances after the end of some rugby club dance in St Ives.

Pam was patient enough to let rugby be part of our honeymoon and we went to Camborne to watch them play a touring side – Roslyn Park – and watched St Ives in their bloody local battle with their rivals, Redruth.

We had a delightful, wonderful fortnight. The weather was kind to us. We wandered round the tiny cobbled streets of St Ives, sat on the quay to watch the fishing boats come in, and explored the almost empty beaches that ran along the coast to the east of St Ives.

Apart from our initial brush with the chambermaid, the service at the hotel was excellent. We could not have wished for anything better. All too soon the fortnight was over and we were packed in my Morris Minor en route for Tadchester to start work as Dr and Mrs Clifford.

Starting married life in Tadchester and sorting out all the presents was like the early days when I first arrived in the town, with leather patches on my jacket and the impoverished look of a newly qualified doctor. I thought then that all the gifts which were showered on me – food, chickens, eggs, loaves of bread, bottles of wine, boxes of chocolates – were in gratitude for my services. It took me some little time to realise that I looked as if I was unable to afford a square meal. There was method in my patients' madness. Having at last got a live doctor, they were going to do their best to keep him that way.

It was the same with a lot of the wedding presents. Fortunately we kept a strict list of what we received from patients, together with their names. We nearly had to develop a card index system. It was well worth doing. Over the next two years, when anyone rang Pam when I was on duty, their requests for a visit would usually be prefaced by, 'Oh, I am Mrs Jones of Mountain Ash Farm. We gave you a vase for your wedding present. It's a tall one with a spiral bottom. I hope Doctor won't be too long in coming.'

The doctor I followed into the practice had only been there briefly for a couple of months when he was sacked because he wouldn't work hard enough. He was one of the first young doctors to take part in the general practitioner training system and he had come into practice with one or two preconceived ideas. These included not seeing more than eight patients a day and putting his car away at five o'clock at night. This did not go down well with my hard-working partners.

Even though his time in the practice was short, Dr Smith still made his mark and was remembered afterwards as the doctor who hypnotized the patients. Having hypnotized one patient, he found at the end of the therapy that he was unable to get her out of her trance. He had to send her to hospital with a diagnosis of 'hypnotic trance – unable to bring the patient round'. That alone was a good enough reason for him to leave Tadchester.

Dr Smith had followed the famous Dr Cooks, who had worked so hard and conscientiously that he set himself standards he could not keep up. He got so involved with patients and their troubles that he would get bogged down with his work and be unable to cope with the volume of it. He emigrated to Canada, hoping to make a fresh start but, being the sort of man he was, he would in no time at all have recreated the situation he had left.

The first home for Pam and myself was a first floor flat in a three-storey house Up-the-Hill. It stood on its own in about a quarter of an acre of garden. The large ground floor flat was occupied by Americans who were tenants of the owner of the house. We were sub-tenants of Herbert Barlow, who rented the top two floors and lived alone in a room on the top floor.

Herbert Barlow was one of the most remarkable and memorable men I have ever met. He was a writer and a man of the theatre. He revelled in the fuss of our settling in and was happy to take messages and to receive graciously the presents that poured in for us. He was a great help when a patient came with a gift. If Pam or I met them, it was sometimes difficult not to ask them in, and once in many of them would have happily stayed all day. Being received by Herbert, with his polished and gracious theatre manners, made them feel they were being treated as very special people.

At one time or another, Herbert had stage managed every London theatre. He had been a script writer in France before the war and had come back into the country to manage the Tadchester repertory theatre. After a break-up of one of his marriages he had devoted his time to play writing, hoping to restore himself to the position that he had once held in the West End. When you knew him well enough to get past the flamboyant stage gestures and flowery language, the man underneath was one of the finest men one could meet, a man of considerable courage and of great personal integrity.

Our week of settling in after our honeymoon passed very

quickly. Almost before I could realise it, I was off to do my first surgery as a married man. It was nice to know that I had my own personal telephone operator when I was on call, that when I came home from work there would be a meal and a welcome waiting for me – and that my routine of eggs or beans on toast was gone for ever.

Apart from the domestic comforts, being married did help to make life in general practice easier. Before I was married there was the tendency to be treated by the older patients as if I were a little boy, by some women patients with female problems with embarrassment and hesitancy, and by my partners – God bless them – as the young lad who was always available because he hadn't the family commitments that they had.

I walked into the consulting room for my first surgery. Gladys, the senior receptionist, was waiting. 'Come on, Dr Bob,' she said, 'the honeymoon is over. Back to work.'

On my desk were piles of hospital letters, medical journals and advertisements from drug houses, which had accumulated during the three weeks that I had been away. It looked comfortingly familiar.

Steve Maxwell came in just before I began to tackle the twenty or so patients, whose names were jotted down on a list before me.

'Nice to see you back, Bob,' he said. 'We've missed you while you have been away. Now don't forget you are a doctor and a married man now, and you are married to your wife and not the practice.'

Steve was probably the wisest and best man I have ever met, and was always able to put his finger on the point of any issue. Many doctors had become so involved with their work and its demands on their time that their marriages had suffered. There was an air of wistfulness about the kindly Steve when he spoke to me in this way. He had always been a bachelor, and he was very firmly married to general practice and his patients. Over the years there must have been many girls who'd set their cap at him, but Steve, being Steve, and knowing himself probably better than any of us would ever know ourselves, realised that there was something in him that would stop him from being able to divide his time equally between a wife and his practice.

I couldn't see that Pam and I would ever have problems in this situation, but I don't expect any young married doctor and his wife, setting out as we did, felt that they would either. I would never be as good a doctor or as wise a man as Steve. It was so good to know that he was keeping an eye on us as a couple, not just me as a doctor-partner. It was a privilege to be able to work with such a man.

*   *   *

My first patient in my first surgery as a married man was Sam Hardcastle. Born in Leeds, exiled in Tadchester, Sam was one of those short-measure conversationalists.

A strange habit among Yorkshiremen, and one which I've noticed in myself now and again, is not finishing the end of a sentence. Whether it's a manifestation of Yorkshire thriftiness, I don't know, but next time you meet a Yorkshireman, listen out for it.

My diagnosis of Sam's ailments was done more by thought reading than by analysis of the spoken word.

Sam would sit down and say, 'Morning, Doctor. I've got a pain in me . . .'

'Leg?'

'No, it's more like me . . .'

'Arm?'

'No, I've just told you. It's more like along me . . .'

'Back?'

'It wouldn't be so bad if it were. You fixed that last time. No, it's a bit more towards . . .'

Eventually, by following Sam's gestures, I would locate the pain. The next thing would be to establish its nature.

'Is it a sharp pain, Sam?'

'No, it's more like a . . .'

'Is it constant? There all the time?'

'No. It's more what you might call . . . It sort of comes and . . .'

'Goes?'

'Hey, that's it! Exactly.'

During one visit I couldn't resist talking back to Sam in the same way.

'Eh, Doctor,' said Sam, 'I'm having a bit of trouble with me . . .'

'I see. With your . . .'

'No. With me . . .'

'Not your. . . ?'

'Yes. Especially in the middle of the . . .'

'During the . . . ?'

'That's it. Gives me terrible cramps in me . . .'

'Oh dear. Does it ever spread to your . . . ?'

'Yes. Gives me gyp, it does.'

'But you've never had it in your . . . ?'

'Not so far, no.'

'Well that's not so bad, I shouldn't worry, Sam, unless it spreads to your . . .'

'Eh, d'you think it might?'

I couldn't contain myself any longer, and burst out laughing. Sam looked bewildered for a moment, then the penny dropped.

'Hey, Doc, you've been kidding. Having me . . .'

'On?'

'That's it. Having me on. Cheeky young . . .'

'Bugger?'

'Bugger . . .'

After that, Sam always made sure he got his story organised and rehearsed before he came to surgery. But after the diagnosis proper we would go into our taciturn Yorkshireman routine for five minutes just for the laughs. Often I'd start:

'Eh, Sam, I aren't half having some trouble with me . . .'

'By heck, that's worrying. Does it ever come out in . . .'

'No, it's more what you might call . . .'

'*Is* it? Have you ever considered having it . . .'

'No, no, Sam. I'm much too attached to it for that. Had it all me . . .'

'As long as that? Think yourself lucky, young man. I've known fellers whose has dropped off first time out . . .'

This would get quite Rabelaisean until in the end I would reveal that I was talking about the exhaust on my car. Sam and I would part with tears rolling down our cheeks. And for both of us, it was a tonic more effective than all the medicines I could prescribe.

*   *   *

Most of the patients who came to surgery that morning had really come to congratulate me. For once most forgot their ills. They seemed to come mainly to be reassured that I hadn't changed now I was married, and things would be as they were.

The slave driver, Gladys, anxious to bed me down in work straight away, had arranged for me to do a long comprehensive medical insurance examination at the end of my surgery. I groaned when I looked at the insurance form. It was the most comprehensive examination that I have ever been called on to do by any insurance company.

My patient, a rather plump, red-cheeked man of forty-three, seemed to have come in determined to enjoy every minute of it. Nobody had ever taken such an interest in his body before. I had to examine eyes, ears, nose, teeth, chest, abdomen, back, limbs, and every orifice that was available to me.

I had to push tubes up him, down him and across him, wherever there was an aperture to enable me to.

At last I finished my tedious and drawn out examination. 'Thank you,' I said to the eager figure on the couch. He had withstood all my pummelling and prodding with a cheerful look on his face. I left him in the cubicle to get dressed, and sat down at my desk to complete his insurance form. I completed it and noticed there had been no movement from behind the curtains since I left the patient, and wondered if he was suffering some reaction to the indignities he had been exposed to.

I gingerly put my head through the curtaining round the couch, and there was the patient, naked except for a pair of socks. He looked up, smiling, and said 'WHAT NEXT, DOCTOR?'

3

Surprise Pictures

There are two routes in and out of Tadchester. The main road from Winchcombe follows first the estuary of the River Trip, turns almost at right angles in the village of Stowin, and runs alongside the estuary of the River Tad into Tadchester.

The other route runs westward from Tadchester Bridge to the small town of Dratchet, about eight miles away. The Dratchet road follows the River Tad right into Dratchet itself.

Three miles out of Tadchester on this route, the river ceases to become tidal. Below this point, in the tidal waters, the fishing rights are free and open to all. Above this point, in the non-tidal waters, both banks are marked off in closely guarded sections for the expensive lease of salmon fishing rights.

It is difficult to say which is the more beautiful of these two approach routes. Each has a character of its own, and contrasting scenery. On the Winchcombe road, you are almost in contact with large expanses of water all the way, with beautiful and changing views of the estuary. The Dratchet road runs through some beautiful countryside, undulating tree-covered hills, and has views over the quiet and gently flowing Tad.

A small railway runs from Tadchester to Dratchet, parallel to the road on the other side of the river. Tadchesterians have always complained that they were cut off from the world on two sides by the sea, and on the other two sides by the railway.

There was a very indifferent train service from Tadchester to

Winchcombe, and a slightly better service from Winchcombe to the outside world: from Winchcombe you could get main line trains to London and various other major cities. The line to Dratchet carried few passengers but was important commercially: a special type of clay was mined in Dratchet and goods trains transported it to the Midlands.

When in later years Dr Beeching axed some of the peripheral train services, the passenger service from Dratchet to Tadchester was closed, but the clay trains were still allowed to chuff their way through to Winchcombe on their way north.

Dratchet was a self-contained community with its own doctors, a small hospital, and a small nursing home, fiercely proud and independent. It tried to have as little to do with Tadchester as possible. Our practice tried similarly to have little to do with Dratchet. There was not much point in a doctor driving eight miles from Tadchester when medical services were there at hand.

There were three single-handed practices in Dratchet, and two of them were real oddities.

Dr Barza settled in Dratchet when there was no real practice to come to. In order to make a living he would take on patients anywhere, never mind the distance. He was quite elderly and lived with his sister. Although based in Dratchet he had patients not only in Tadchester, but in Winchcombe and all over the place. I would be coming back from a visit late at night and see him visiting in Tadchester, and at eight o'clock in the morning would sometimes see him doing routine calls.

There were all sorts of tales about him, some of them true. It was said that it was one of his practices to say to a patient with a headache, after a brief examination, that he had a cerebral tumour. He would say, 'You have come just in time,' and give him some tablets – privately of course.

Two or three months later, after some expensive treatment, he would pronounce his patient cured. You could safely say that there were more cured cerebral tumours in Dratchet than any other place in the world.

The other eccentric Dratchet doctor, and the best known and

most loved, was Dr Knight. Dr Knight's first love was a bottle of whisky. There is something about doctors who are addicted to alcohol. Patients adore them. They make any excuse for them when they are incapacitated by drink, and always say, 'My God, what wonderful doctors they are when they are sober.'

Perhaps people assume that alcoholic doctors are the most sensitive and human of all. That they know what life is really all about, and feel that the only sensible thing to do is to kill the pain with drink all the time.

Dr Knight met his come-uppance when in Tadchester one market day he had too much to drink at the Tadchester Arms and the landlord refused to give him any more. Infuriated by this impertinence, Dr Knight jumped into his car and drove to the police station to report the landlord. Of course he was accused of being drunk in charge of a motor vehicle and eventually disqualified from driving for a year. For that year he had to have a man to drive him around – and this enabled him to drink even more.

There were many stories about Dr Knight and his boozing. The hospital secretary, visiting his home after some hospital Christmas function, was offered a drink of whisky. 'There were only five of us,' he said, 'but a third bottle had to be broached to complete the pouring of one round.'

Dr Knight was a great advertisement for the staying power of alcohol. He was still running his general practice at the age of eighty, and was still the well-loved and well-respected general practitioner. The patients used to say 'Our old doc. will go on for ever, and will never need embalming. He has been completely pickled for the last thirty years.'

Although we discouraged patients living in and near Dratchet from joining our practice, it was very difficult to strike off patients we had looked after for many years and who moved out there.

Doris and Bill Slewman, husband and wife, were two such patients. They had had one of the roughest, dirtiest old farms Up-the-Hill, about five miles from Tadchester. Now they had moved to a dirty, tumbledown cottage, six miles west of

Tadchester, in a field two miles to the east of Dratchet. It had no amenities, such as running water or inside plumbing, and Doris, who'd worked all her life and was now getting on, reckoned she'd at last earned a sit down.

Although I was called to the cottage many times over many years, I never ever saw Doris move from her chair. She used to sit there, looking out through the door over the fields, with a small clay pipe clenched between her teeth, and an old battered radio playing at her side.

I had some evidence that she did move occasionally. One day I sat down in a chair next to her, only to discover when I got up that the seat of my trousers was decidedly damp. Doris had so determined to rest and put her feet up when they gave up the farm, that now she wouldn't even leave her chair to go to the toilet.

Somehow she lived on, refused any medical care, became steadily more odoriferous as the years went by. She reluctantly agreed for the district nurse to give her a wash once a week, and lived on to a great age. In spite of the fact that she sat in a pool of her own product most of the day, she never ever got a bed sore.

The one luxury the Slewmans had in the cottage was a telephone. This was needed for Bill's calls to the doctor. Bill was unlike Doris. Whereas she had no difficulty in passing water, which was obvious from the state of the saturated chairs, Bill's problem was that from time to time he 'got stuck'.

Men who get stuck, who cannot pass water, have to have their prostate gland removed. Once you have inserted a catheter and emptied the bladder, the bladder will block off again unless the gland is removed, or so I was told as a medical student. Bill's case defied the teaching. After his bladder had been emptied, he would often manage to remain unblocked for two or three months.

Bill, who had to be intermittently unblocked for several years, suddenly changed to not blocking off at all, and wandered around wetting everything as if he was (in fact he *was*) carrying his own personal stream around with him.

'You've got to do something about it,' said Doris from the depths of what I suspected was her own urine-soaked chair. 'We're going to be washed out of the house.'

I was at a loss to know what to do. On one occasion I had to dissuade Bill from putting a clothes peg on his offending member. In despair, I went to consult Neville Jackson who ran the Tadchester chemist's. I asked if there was anything on the National Health that might help this situation.

'Yes,' said Neville. 'The best buy, that is the best give away, is a portable male urinal.'

He fished behind the counter and brought out a thing that looked like a pair of gun holsters with a balloon in front and a tube leading off to another balloon below. It really was a most ingenious piece of plumbing.

I took it straight round to Bill and between us we strapped it on him. He had to insert himself into a tube that led into a bag through which another tube passed to a further bag that had a strap to go round his ankle. The whole apparatus was fixed on by a combination of rubber and webbing, and was anchored firmly by a belt round the waist.

Bill thought it was marvellous. He said 'When I'm int'

market, doctor, all I've got to do is to stand by the street drain and open me bottom tap. Nobody will know what I'm doing.'

It worked like a charm. Bill was very happy with his new device. I only wished there was one that his wife could have worn. But you can't win them all.

*　　　*　　　*

I only knew general practice or, in fact, medicine, after it became nationalised. Although the nationalised branch of medicine had been going for a few years by the time I went into practice, patients hadn't fully explored all its possibilities. They were still testing and trying this new unbelievable toy which was all theirs for absolutely nothing. Some felt that they now employed doctors and treated them very much in that way. Many, particularly the well-off, accepted the National Health Service as a great blessing – free universal medicine for all – but still expected to get private and personal treatment. The doctor must understand that they were rather different.

Steve Maxwell said that in the old days there were those who paid, those who were always about to pay, and those who never paid at all. The commonest delaying tactic was 'Oh, we will be killing a pig in the next week or two, and will settle up then, Doctor.'

The semi-rural area in which the Tadchester practice was situated benefited to some extent by these changes. So many people in the farming community were used to paying in kind at Christmas. After the inauguration of the National Health Service, their doctors still received a tremendous amount of produce – drink, chickens, turkeys and geese. The farmers who had always paid bills just couldn't believe these medical services were for nothing.

For the patients who never ever paid bills, the abundant munificence of the National Health Service was overwhelming. So many things could be obtained for nothing if you knew how. These included plastic anklets which could keep the feet warm in winter; elastic stockings, both full length and below the knee

– these could either be nylon yarn for the winter or fine nylon for the summer; hernia trusses; corsets, both boned and unboned; plastic knickers; surgical brassieres and any amount of cotton-wool. Lengths of gauze substituted very well for net curtains. False teeth, glasses, wigs and hearing aids were all standard. There were various ancillary services such as aids for getting in and out of your bath, special elevated seats for toilets, and extra food for special diets. Also available was extra money for special heating and insulation where the patient's medical condition required a warm or draught-free atmosphere.

It was no surprise to me when Fred Bowen came to the surgery. Fred had had chronic asthma and bronchitis for many years. He was not a severe case, but he was to a certain extent handicapped by recurrent chest infections, especially in the winter. He came to the surgery looking relatively well, and his request was not for medicine.

'It's like this, Doctor,' he said. 'When I goes up from the lounge to me bedroom; the cold air in me bedroom makes me lungs go into spasm and I can't get me breath. If you gives me a letter to take to the Social Security, they will put a gas fire in me bedroom and help pay the bill.'

Always happy to take the least line of resistance in these cases, I dutifully gave Fred his chitty. As he was leaving the consulting room I noticed some big, round object hanging from his hand by a strap.

'What's that?' I asked.

'Oh,' said Fred, 'that's a crash helmet.'

'Whatever do you want with a crash helmet?'

'Well,' said Fred, a bit sheepishly, 'I have just bought meself a motorbike. I get a bit breathless climbing these hills.'

I exploded . . .

*　　　*　　　*

Fred's motorbike didn't last long, and for some reason he didn't get his gas fire installed. His chest got progressively worse and he had to spend quite a lot of time at home. He was too breathless

31

to get out, particularly when he had one of his recurrent infections.

When I called one day I noticed him painting with poster paints in an exercise book. This was a great surprise to me as I had never had the highest opinion of Fred's application. I found that he had about a dozen exercise books filled with carefully executed primitive paintings. They had a special quality all their own. Although by some standards they could be judged as childish, they obviously illustrated what the artist meant to show. A house was a house even if it was out of proportion with the rest of the landscape; a tractor was a tractor; a car was a car, even though a dog in the same picture could easily be as big as the car. I knew nothing about painting, but felt that Fred had some particular quality in his work and that, as a therapy at least, he should be encouraged.

'I wish I could have some lessons,' said Fred. 'I've always wanted to paint in oils.'

We had in Tadchester a very well-known artist, John Floyd. He was successful in that he had seven children whom he managed to send to private school, two houses and a gallery, all of which he supported by his paintings. He was one of the few successful, or at least economically successful, painters that I have met. Many of his more important works were exhibited in London.

I asked if he would come and cast an eye over Fred's work and perhaps give him some instruction and encouragement.

When he had seen some of Fred's paintings he said, 'I can't instruct him. I wouldn't dream of interfering with what he does. He is a natural, primitive artist of the highest calibre. I'll just show him a bit about oils, but I wouldn't dream of trying in any way to give him instruction.'

So, with the encouragement of myself and John Floyd, Fred started to do one or two oil paintings on canvas. There was something very engaging about his work. We encouraged him to enter some paintings for the exhibition by Tadchester artists at the Humber Memorial Art Gallery, situated in the park just off the Tadchester Quay.

Tadchester had an art gallery which was much better and much larger than one would have expected for a town of its size and situation. Charles Humber had been a successful son of Tadchester, who had made money abroad, come back and built the Humber Art Gallery as a memorial to himself.

For two weeks in the summer the Tadchester Art Society, a very snooty, tight little circle of people, held its own exhibition at the gallery, when paintings by the members were put on show for possible sale. Non-members too were allowed to submit paintings for consideration, and the successful paintings were exhibited in a room set aside specially for the purpose. With our encouragement, Fred entered four. Two, with pressure, were very reluctantly accepted by the Art Society and were hung in the gallery. In the exhibition catalogue one was priced at £5 and the other at £7.

Fred, his wife and his daughter, all bursting with pride, went down every day hoping to see the red stamps on the paintings which would indicate that they had been sold.

With two days of the exhibition still to go, neither of Fred's pictures had been sold. I started to worry. I knew that Fred needed the encouragement of a sale to involve him seriously with painting. John Floyd had stressed that Fred must persevere with his particular style to develop his quite exceptional talent.

Then I made the mistake of doing what is so easy to do as a GP – of trying to play God. Being so pleased that through my perceptive, artistic intuition I had discovered an artist, I couldn't let it stop there. I anonymously bought the less expensive of the two paintings. I couldn't have it delivered to my house, so I rang up my old friend Bob Barker, who kept the bookshop at Sanford-on-Sea, explaining the situation, and asking would he mind if the picture were delivered to him.

Bob chuckled. 'Playing God again,' he said. 'It will land you in trouble one day. Yes, I can put it away in a corner of the shop somewhere, particularly somewhere I don't have to look at it.'

So it was arranged that the painting should be delivered to

Bob Barker's bookshop.

The Bowens were overcome and bursting with excitement that one of Fred's pictures had been sold. They pestered and re-pestered the Art Society committee to find out who had bought it. Eventually they managed to drag out from one of the officials that the picture had gone to Bob Barker's bookshop at Sanford-on-Sea.

They gleefully told me their story when I next visited them. I had to appear surprised, and congratulated Fred.

Fred now really got down to work with a will, and was soon producing a painting every other day. I had to examine them all and make comments on his latest product every time I called.

There was an air of success and happiness around the house, and I was pleased with myself that a lot of this was due to my efforts.

It was my habit once a week, or at the very least once a fort-night, to slip away from my work to Barker's Bookshop and spend some time with dear old Bob, who kept a small box of cigars in his desk drawer for my visits. We explored whole areas of literature together, and put the world to rights. It was an as-sociation I treasured, and a man for whom I had tremendous admiration. When I visited him a week after the art exhibition, I had a welcome that for the first time was less than cordial. Bob was, if anything, a bit grumpy. He looked at me, nodding over his glasses.

'Good afternoon, God,' he said. 'I don't want to get mixed up in your good works again.' And with a twinkle in his eye he told me he had had to call into a shop in town. It happened to be the butcher's. His wife was picking up the meat and he was idly gazing out of the window when a young woman came round the counter and asked if he was Bob Barker. When he confirmed that he was, she almost got on the ground to kiss his feet. She was apparently Fred Bowen's daughter. With tears in her eyes, she told Bob Barker how much difference his buying her father's painting had made to all their lives. What a fine, won-derful man he was, and how generous and perceptive. No adjec-tive was too extravagant for her to use in his praise.

'You see what you let me in for,' he said. 'Now here is £5. I couldn't possibly accept the painting for nothing. I have got to pay for it, having all this goodwill heaped on me. I hate the bloody painting and have hidden it behind the cupboard. So just keep me out of any further of your projects please Dr Bob.' (With both of us being Bobs, my name was always given a handle by Bob Barker, close friends though we were.)

Bob Barker had no malice, and his bad temper was only pretence. We had a good laugh over it. It was a lesson to me. It is so easy being clever, playing with people's lives.

Fred Bowen did stick at his painting. He began to sell pictures here and there, entered more local exhibitions. In all he perhaps sold seventy to eighty paintings, enough to cover the cost of materials, his canvases, paints, brushes, and to bring the family a small amount of money. Not enough to make any real difference to his life style, but enough to buy a few small comforts and give him some standing.

Fred's painting gave him pride and a place in the community. After being a nonentity for many years he was now a somebody. The height of his artistic career was reached when Western Television screened an art summer series each week, showing on the programme the work of an artist from the west of England. For one week Fred Bowen's paintings were shown – a different painting each night – as the work of an established West Country artist.

Over two or three years Fred reached heights of achievement that one would never have thought possible. He did this in spite of ill health. He never had a lesson. He was never internationally famous, but before he died, he'd sold about a hundred paintings. The most he ever got for one was £40, and the majority sold for about £10 or £15. But what was important was that he changed from being a nobody into a somebody.

The chest condition which had bothered him for so many years had begun to throw a strain on his heart. Eventually his heart could cope no longer. About six months after his paintings had appeared on television, he died. But he did not die as Fred Bowen of 63 North Street, Tadchester. He died as Fred

Bowen, the well-known artist, whose paintings had been shown on television. There is no better accolade in this day and age than to appear on television.

Over the years Fred had given me some of his paintings, which I kept, telling him I expected that one day they would be worth a great deal of money. And I noticed, although I never mentioned it, that the painting that Bob Barker had so unwillingly bought was placed in a prominent position in his shop soon after the television appearances of Fred's other paintings. Even wise, dear old Bob was as susceptible to conversion by the media as anyone else . . .

AS SEEN ON TV
(AND BOUGHT BY GOD)

4

Visitors

Pam settled down very happily in Tadchester. As we were by the sea, we had an unending stream of visitors. We were surprised how popular we had become with friends in London now that we lived and could provide accommodation for them in the glorious countryside and seaside of Tadchester and Sanford-on-Sea.

Younger friends loved to go seine net fishing with us in the surf at Sanford-on-Sea. There was something fundamental and satisfying about wading through the breakers, tugging a net and catching one's own food: certainly a contrast to London life.

Pam explored all the Tadchester shops with her friend Zara. Zara always had an eye for a bargain and knew all the little out-of-the-way places where the best things could be had. As well as the shops there was the huge covered pannier market to which the country people brought such assorted produce as fruit, vegetables, preserves, pickles and flowers.

We were fortunate that we lived next door to Fred Derrigan. Fred had a smallholding where he grew vegetables, and a few glasshouses where he grew tomatoes, raspberries and strawberries. He was a big, stoical man, and wicket keeper in one of the village cricket teams. He kept us constantly supplied with vegetables. I am sure that they were at a reduced price. Anyway Pam found that housekeeping was cheaper than she thought it would be.

It was Pam who called me urgently to see Fred one morning. 'Come quickly,' she said. 'I think Fred's dying.' Pam had still not yet got used to people with medical conditions.

When I reached Fred he certainly looked in a bad way.

'I feel as if I am going to die, Doc,' he said. 'I have a tremendous pain in my side, it's the worst I have ever had. The pain is really terrible. It goes down into my left testicle.'

Fred was in obvious distress. As I questioned him further I found that he'd been passing water more frequently. He really did look a sorry sight. I examined him, and could find nothing wrong, except that he was a bit tender in his left testicle.

'Well, Doctor?' said Fred as I finished my examination.

'I think, Fred,' I said, 'you've got what we call a ureteric calculus. This means a little stony crystal is trying to pass down the tube from your kidney to your bladder. It is one of the most painful conditions there is. I shall want a specimen of urine from you, and I shall want you to look to see if you pass any bits of gravel. I'm going to give you an injection now that not only relieves pain but also relieves the spasm of the little tube that's got the crystal in it and helps to pass it along.'

I explained that the most common cause of these stones was oxalic acid crystallising out in the kidney, and the kidney trying to pass the crystals down to the bladder. This is more common in hot climates where there has been excessive sweating and the urine becomes concentrated, but if you eat a lot of fruit which contains oxalic acid, like tomatoes or strawberries, it is much more likely to happen. Sometimes the crystals form without there being any apparent outside factor.

'Look out for stones, Fred,' I said. 'And if the pain gets very bad again, give me a ring. Drink plenty of water and bring in a sample tomorrow. If you should start passing blood in your water, don't worry: it often happens in this condition.'

Fred called me during the night, in absolute agony. I had to give him an injection of pethedin. The next day he was up, perfectly fit again. His urine sample showed some blood cells in it, but no sign of infection.

I saw no more of Fred for two days after my night visit until

38

he came beaming into the surgery with a small jagged crystal in his hand.

'Here it is, Doc' he said. 'I've laid an egg. Is that it now?'

'I think so,' I replied. 'What we have to do now, Fred, is to have a special x-ray of your waterworks just to see if there are any other stones left that might be blocking off your kidney. Some dye will be injected into your blood stream and pictures taken of the dye as it passes through your kidney down the tube from the kidney to the bladder. It's called, if it's any help to you, an intravenous pylogram.'

After his x-ray Fred came to the surgery for the result. It was quite clear.

'I must say, Doc,' said Fred, 'I had been bashing the strawberries a bit. I've grown them under glass this year and have been eating them all the time. You know what my wife is saying now – "People who work in glass houses shouldn't grow stones".'

After Fred's kidney incident we found that our vegetables got even cheaper still. He almost gave us our tomatoes and strawberries for nothing. This was a tremendous help to Pam as the summer came along, when we had even more visitors coming to see us and the seaside at the same time.

*   *   *

Two of our first visitors in our new home were Herbert and Margaret Hodge. Herbert had had a stroke and was unable to drive, so I drove across to Hastings to fetch them.

Herbert and I had struck up a friendship from appearing together on a TV show when I was down the coal mines just after the end of the war. It was a topical magazine programme and I got a telegram to ask if I would appear. I am still trying to work out why.

When I first met Herbert he was in the peak of his achievements. He was a taxi driver who'd become a very well-known writer and broadcaster. He had written several books including *A Cockney on Main Street,* about his adventures in America where the Ministry of Labour had sent him lecturing during the war, and other books about the cab trade.

His life read like a book. He'd come from a poor, but scrupulously honest background. After his mother died, he had gone steerage with the insurance money to Canada by cattle boat. In Canada he had worked on the railways, as a lumberjack, and as a firefighter in the timber forests. He had then come back to England, worked in a garage, and progressed to become a cab driver and chauffeur.

Sitting in the cab ranks, he began to scribble, and his first articles were accepted for magazines like *Cab Trade News.* Then he wrote two plays, *Cannibal Carnival* and *Where's that Bomb?* These were political plays performed at the Unity Theatre, and were subsequently taken up and performed by the Oxford and Cambridge Dramatic Society in England and the Harvard and Yale Dramatic Society in America.

A big, heavily built man, Herbert was one of the most fundamentally honest men that I have ever met. He took up any new experience, shook it like a terrier and explored it to a degree. After our first meeting he took me to a cab shelter, a wooden shed with a steaming stove in the corner. There, sitting jammed among the cabbies, I learnt some of their terminology – a new cab driver was a butter boy, for instance – and all about the gruelling examinations they had to go through on the geography of London streets before they could pass as a London cabby.

One of Herbert's books *It's Draughty up Front* was autobiographical: the title came from the fact that the cab driver had to sit at the front, uncovered and exposed to the elements. In this book Herbert described his life outside his work and his various stages of exploration and education.

He began in his late teens by being caught up with religious fervour, exploring one denomination after another, and finally giving this up in order to become a communist. He went from communism to fascism, joining Mosley's Party, gradually getting disillusioned with it, but not until he had stood as a Mosley candidate in the East End against Clement Attlee.

He then became an ardent and potentially lifelong socialist and was absolutely thrilled when the first post-war government was Labour. He said somehow it all seemed too good to be true. He wondered whether all their wonderful socialist ideas would work. In his latter life he considered that they hadn't.

He said, 'I hate to confess it, but now that I have a little bit of money, I worry about it, whereas I was never worried about it before. If anybody classified me now, I expect I am a conservative.'

Herbert's literary achievements steadily grew and he became a well-known figure, both as a writer and broadcaster. He wrote three major hard-back books: *Cab Sir?*, *It's Draughty up Front*, and *A Cockney on Main Street*. He'd had both his plays produced, he started doing radio for a magazine programme called *London Town,* and his broadcasts on London were used in commonwealth schools to teach children about London. He wrote a great number of articles for various magazines and journals and was approached by *John Bull* magazine. He was asked by them to come and see them, but kept on putting it off. Eventually they offered him £5 expenses to go and see them, and this resulted in Herbert writing a thousand-word weekly column: a friendly, philosophical column which ran for a period of about ten years. In the meantime he had also become the theatre and film critic for *John o' London's Weekly*.

A couple of years after I met him he had his first stroke. I think what had happened was that Herbert had written himself out. He was so honest that if he had written something once,

41

then he couldn't write it or use it again; he had to find fresh material each time to put fresh ideas forward. Over ten years it is very difficult to find fresh ideas for a column every week. I think that he had exhausted himself completely, mentally and physically. As well as his column, which took most of his time and energy, he was lecturing for libraries and at one time did some two-way transatlantic broadcasts with Alistair Cooke.

The fresh air of Tadchester seemed to revive him. He seemed to have more use in his paralysed limb – he even drove my car for a while – and he went back after a holiday all fired to write. But it was as if nature had said, 'You've done all you can; there is no more writing left in you.' As soon as he had started to write again he had a further stroke which prevented both writing and typing.

Round about this time Radio Luxembourg did a *This is Your Life* programme about Herbert, and in lieu of a fee presented him with a tape recorder. This meant that although he couldn't write, he could speak into a tape recorder. For some years up until his death we carried on discussions and arguments on the tapes.

His was a friendship that I valued greatly, and I was heartbroken that it had to end so soon. But he was one of several cases that I came to see in my years in practice; when someone had given all they had to give, their body stopped them from doing any more. If Herbert had written anything else it could have been only repetition of previous works and he just wasn't this sort of animal. I took the best, or what I thought the best, of the hundreds of philosophical workaday articles like *To Doubt is to Discover* and put them away. I hope that one day I might be able to bring them out and that somebody might be interested enough to give them a second reading.

5

Fishy Business

I was always glad to bump into John Denton, the River Authority bailiff on the Tadchester end of the River Tad.

Born and raised in the industrial North, in an atmosphere he described as three parts sulphur dioxide and four parts muck, he had opted for the country life after his wartime army service and eventually finished up in Tadchester.

Big, bluff, boozy, gregarious, he was a dedicated bailiff and angler and the scourge of the local poachers. Patient as a saint with youngsters or inexperienced anglers, he took no nonsense from anybody trying to pull the wool over his eyes; especially the superior county types who, as he so delicately put it, got on his bloody wick.

He came into surgery one morning in the summer with a bandaged finger.

'Mornin', Bob,' he said. 'How are you?'

'All the better for seeing you, John. But I'm supposed to be asking the questions. How are *you*? And what have you done to your finger?'

'Bloody mink,' he said.

This was John. He seldom needed my professional services, but when he did it was always for something bizarre. The first time I treated him was for the removal of a salmon lure which a clumsy pupil had managed to hook very firmly into John's giant rump.

'Mink?' I said. 'Of course. There's a lot of it about. You're the tenth case of minkitis this morning.'

'No, Bob, I'm not kidding. Took a mink out of a trap this morning and the little bugger nearly had my finger off.'

He unwrapped the bandage. The top half of his finger gave a passable imitation of freshly minced steak.

As I cleaned and dressed the wound, or rather wounds, and prepared an anti-tetanus injection, John told me the story.

The banks of the Tad were plagued by mink, wild mink augmented by cross-breeding with escapees from the local mink farm. Beautiful animals, they ranged in colour from black to golden brown, and some of the fully grown males were almost the size of an otter.

They gave John a lot of problems. Incredibly fast, fierce and vicious, they wreaked havoc among the water birds and the fish. More than a match for the normal natural predators, they were also prolific breeders. Without John's intervention they would have ruined the balance of wildlife along the river, let alone the fishing.

John kept their numbers down with shotgun and traps. The trapping was done with humane catch-'em-alive traps. Instead of drowning the mink inside the traps, or shooting them through the bars with a .22 pistol, John preferred to take the catches to the mink farm. There, those with unsuitable pelts would be painlessly gassed. Those with marketable pelts would stay for a short but happy life of non-stop eating until they grew to full size.

The mink farm manager was happy to do this: it eased his conscience about the inevitable number of escapees which were constantly adding to John's problems. John was happy: the mink were put down painlessly, and he made a bit of beer money from the sale of the pelts. There was even a market for odd-coloured or unmatchable pelts as fun furs in the local gift shops.

'Any road,' said John, 'I had this mink in the trap this morning. A big 'un. And a lovely colour. I didn't have my leather gloves with me, and like a fool I took it out to put it in a sack barehanded. Thought I was used enough to 'em by now. Know all, know nowt, me mam used to say.'

John waxed lyrical about the qualities of mink. Beautiful, voracious, aggressive, fearless, passionate as lovers and devoted as parents.

'There was this pair in the spring,' he mused. 'Courting. Doing this funny little dance, running round and round each other, making all sorts of loops and twirls, getting faster and faster. All happening on the bank, with the morning sun making their coats shine like polished gold. They went faster and faster and faster, moving closer to each other all the time. And then they clutched each other in this sort of embrace for the actual mating . . .'

'Oh, that's beautiful, John.'

'Then I shot 'em. Pair of 'em. With one barrel of me twelve-bore. Broke me heart. But what a way to go . . .'

*　　*　　*

John's tales of fish and fishermen made me decide to take up the sport. As a boy, of course, I had tried the bent-pin-and-string techniques, but boxing and rugby took over in my early teens, girls took over in my later teens, and from then on my leisure time was fully occupied.

I fancied game fishing – fly fishing for salmon and trout – with all the mystique which seemed to attend the pursuit of these two fish. But John said, 'Nay lad. You'll start where you ought: with coarse fishing. You'll learn to use a rod properly, learn how to read a water, learn how to use cover. And then you can move on to the fly.'

Coarse fishing didn't sound right to me. Certainly I had heard many of the tweedy game fishermen sneering at coarse anglers.

'Take no notice,' said John. 'Coarse doesn't mean *coarse*. There are techniques in coarse fishing which are much more refined than half these tweedy buggers could use. There are hooks so small you can hardly see to put the bait on, and line so fine that it's almost invisible.'

He explained that the origins of the word *coarse*, applied to fish, were obscure. As far as he had been able to discover, the word came from the old phrase *in course*, which meant in the normal run of things, ordinary, i.e. every freshwater fish except salmon and trout.

John was a true angler, an all-round fisherman for whom every fish had its own special magic, and every technique its own special application. He had no patience with the 'dray flay mob', as he called them, who brayed every evening in the Tadchester Arms about the delicate art of fly fishing being the only occupation for an officer and a gentleman.

'See him,' he said one night, indicating an elderly man in sober tweeds, quietly drinking in a corner of the bar. 'Ex-colonial governor, he is. Can run rings round these bluffers with any bait you like. Pulled out a salmon last year which was damn near the record for the river. Yet he's as happy as Larry going for pike and carp as well. If anybody wants advice, he'll give it. Otherwise he keeps himself to himself, probably for fear of bursting out laughing. He's spit better fishermen than this lot before breakfast.'

'I say, Denton,' brayed one of the chinless wonders. 'We're trying the pool at Robbins' Reach tomorrow. What do you think of our chances?'

John bristled. He was paid as a bailiff, but the terms of employment did not include having the handle left off his name. With a great effort of self-control he turned calmly to face his questioner.

'If you can catch fish,' he said quietly, 'you'll be all right at Robbins' Reach.'

'Ah, thank you, Denton. Hear that, chaps? We should do well tomorrow.'

'Don't know why I bother,' muttered John. 'Sarcasm's wasted on this lot. Tell you what, Bob. Tomorrow I'll show you two fishermen at opposite ends of the scale. Then you'll begin to see what I mean.'

*　　　*　　　*

At six next morning I joined John at the gates of the fish farm. The farm bred trout for the restaurant trade, and both trout and coarse fish for periodic stockings of the river. Running the farm was part of John's duties.

Trout which had grown beyond the optimum restaurant size, or those which were surplus at any given time, were put into a stock pond. Anglers were allowed to fish the pond for a moderate fee, and were restricted to a brace of trout each.

John led the way to the stock pond. In the middle of the pond stood the archetypal trout fisherman: waders, tweed jacket, creel over his shoulder, short-handled net looped in his belt, a tweed hat festooned with trout flies, and swishing a rod back and forth over his shoulder as he paid out line.

He looked up as we approached.

'Ah. Morning, Denton.'

'Another of 'em,' muttered John. 'Ignorant buggers.' Then, 'Morning, Colonel. How's your luck?'

'Not too good, I'm afraid. Little devils playing hard to get this morning. Still, a bit of sun on the water and I'll have the blighters.'

'I'm sure you will, sir,' said John. 'No more than two, mind.'

'Dammit, man, what do you take me for?' bellowed the Colonel.

'A bloody idiot,' said John quietly as we turned away. 'Ex-Indian Army, that one. Pride of the Bengal Prancers. Comes here every year, done up to the nines, and fishes the stock pond with a dry fly. Won't use anything else.'

John explained that a dry fly floats on the water, and is only effective on gin-clear runs at certain times when natural flies are hatching.

'He's fishing a pond of murky water. A bloody sight murkier by the time he's finished wading all over it. And for trout which have been hand fed on bloody great protein pellets and wouldn't know a dry fly if they saw one. He'll fish it every day for a week, catch nowt, and then complain in his club that fishing in England has never been the same since we lost India. But he knows that nobody but a bounder would use anything else but dray flay.'

'What would you use, John?'

'Small spinner. Big, heavy, wet fly. If nobody was looking, a bloody great lobworm.'

'Why if nobody was looking?'

'Against the rules. Too easy. We like the customers to get their money's worth. And two trout in five minutes is hardly cricket, what? Come on, lad, and I'll show you the other kind of fisherman: the real one.'

We approached the bank of the Tad.

'Take it quietly from here, Bob,' whispered John. 'Follow me, single file, and don't step on any twigs.'

We crept up to the bank and peered from behind some foliage.

'There he is,' hissed John. 'Dead opposite on the other bank.'

'I can't see anybody,' I whispered.

'Exactly. That's a real fisherman. Now watch this.'

He cupped his hands to his mouth and bellowed:

'Out of there, you little bugger – I can see you! I'll be over in my boat in a minute and tan your backside! Go on – out of it!'

There was a scurry in the undergrowth on the opposite bank, a glimpse of a tousled head of sun-bleached hair, and the flash of two fresh-caught fish strung by the gills. Then silence. And not another movement.

'He'll go far, that lad,' said John. 'Tommy Thompson. Best little poacher for miles.'

'What will you do about him?'

'Nowt. That's the rules. He's a lucky lad, growing up in the country. Goes ferreting for rabbits. Got a little terrier for rats. And a rod that's no more than a hazel twig with six feet of line on the end. See those fish he had? Trout. Good 'uns.

'With lads like that, the rules are that I make a lot of noise and they clear off.'

'And I thought you were a hard man.'

'I am that,' said John. 'Hard as bloody putty . . .'

*   *   *

My fishing career was due to start on the first day of the coarse fishing season: June 16th. For a couple of weeks beforehand, John loaned me a set of tackle and gave me some lessons on dry land in the field behind his cottage.

He taught me how to assemble the rod from the top joint downwards; take it apart from the bottom joint upwards. How to 'sight' along the rings of an assembled rod to make sure they were all in a straight line. How to cast, first with a centre-pin reel – the 'wheel' type – and then with the more sophisticated fixed-spool type. He had me casting both for distance and accuracy, using weights but no hooks on the end of the line. Though I say it myself, I became pretty good at both. He taught how to 'strike' – how to lift the rod with a smart wrist action to set the hook in the fish's mouth, yet to do no more than that to avoid damage to the fish.

John even taught me how to play a fish, with himself as the catch. With the end of the line in a gloved hand – the fine nylon could cut like a knife into bare skin – he would lumber about in imitation of the fish's diving and turning movements and bellow instructions.

'Keep the rod up – up, you silly bugger! Now give it line! Now turn its head at the top of the run . . . sidestrain! Drop the rod tip and turn it! Now bring it back towards you . . . even pressure . . . steady as she goes . . . Now the landing net . . . into the water. Always fish to net, never net to fish. Right . . . net in the water – now bring me in. Gently . . . I'm knackered, but I still might kick at the last knockings. Gently . . . over the net –' and here he would clomp one of his size ten wellies into the landing net '– and hup!'

All this would have looked silly enough if anybody had been around to watch it – and certainly the cows in the field looked pretty bewildered by it all – but it was nothing to John's lessons on approaching the water.

I had to assemble the rod away from the bank, and leave it behind while I took the big wicker fishing basket down to 'set out my stall', as John put it. The approach to the water was done at a crouch, keeping below the skyline, using cover in front

of me and behind me, and in one or two exposed places even in a commando crawl.

This looked ridiculous – and on one occasion came as a great shock to a courting couple – but it was necessary if one was not to frighten the fish away. Fish can see a surprising distance above the surface, can register bright colours or flashes of light and will shy away at sudden movements, unfamiliar objects on the skyline, or shadows. So clothes had to be drab, movements slow, and posture low.

'Looks daft, Bob,' said John. 'Let's face it – it is daft. But we're *stalking* the fish. They're not very bright, but they survive by clearing off at the first sign of anything they're not used to. The best kind of fisherman is the one you don't see – like the lad we chased off the other week. And don't forget: the fish can *feel* vibrations very keenly. So tread softly. Don't go clumping about in your bloody great boots.'

Setting out the stall meant unpacking the gear from the basket, placing rod rests gently but firmly into the bank, putting bait tins and bags of groundbait within easy reach, staking out the keepnet in the shade, and assembling the landing net before any thought of fishing.

'Never forget that, Bob,' said John. 'Always assemble the landing net first, no matter what fish are moving, no matter how excited you are. I've lost count of the loonies – and even experienced fishermen – who have had a damn great fish on and then had nowt to land it with.'

*　　　*　　　*

June 16th was traditionally the time for tench. John didn't tell me, but a week before he had dragged a v-shaped path through a bed of weed in the river. Every night for that week he had thrown groundbait into the cleared swim. So unless I did something horribly wrong, I couldn't fail. But, as John said later, 'There's no start like a good start, Bob. And there's nowt better to start with than tench.'

The magic of that misty summer morning is still with me. Just the tip of my float was showing above the almost still water of a gentle green eddy. The only movement was that of a vole which fussed across to the bank, climbed out, shook itself, had a scratch, and then ambled off without even noticing the presence of the two humans. A robin perched cheekily on the end of my rod, then hopped down to filch a couple of maggots from the bait tin.

Nothing happened. Nothing . . . Until, 'Here they come, Bob. See those bubbles . . .'

In several parts of the cleared swim rose dead straight lines of tiny bubbles.

'Feeding tench,' whispered John. 'Always thousands of tiny bubbles in straight lines. With bream you get fewer bubbles, but bigger. And wobbly. With carp, bigger bubbles still. And with both of them, clouds of mud. But with tench, dead straight lines of . . . eh, watch your float, lad . . .'

The tip of my float had trembled ever so slightly.

'Give it time,' said John. 'Tench are fiddlers. Be ready, but there's no rush. It'll pick up the bait and lift the float. Then the float will lie flat on the surface. Then it will slide under. When it slides under, strike . . .'

After what seemed an age of trembling and fiddling, the float rose in the water. Then it keeled over and lay flat. Then it slid gently under . . . strike!

No amount of theorising can prepare you for the thrill of a real fish, especially such a fish as a tench, whose broad, powerful tail gives it a remorseless forward thrust. No fireworks, such as you get with pike or trout; no darting, jagging fight; no head-shaking leaps out of the water . . . just a steady, seemingly unstoppable thrust.

Thanks to John's previous instructions, and to his whispered 'Don't panic. Keep your rod up. Turn him at those weeds . . .' I kept in contact with the fish and eventually drew it over the landing net. Hup! And there it was . . . a magical, green-bronze, compact bundle of muscle with an eye of African gold.

I had six tench that morning. No spectacular weights, as I learned later – each around the three and a half-pound mark – but to me they were the biggest and most beautiful fish in the world.

The only thing I wasn't keen on was their slime: thick, glutinous and plenty of it. John told me of the legend of the Doctor Fish: that pike were supposed not to eat tench, in return for being allowed to rub their wounds against the tench's healing slime.

'Do you reckon that's true, John?'

'Couldn't say, Bob. If it is, the pike I've opened up can't have spent much time listening to old wives' tales . . .'

*　　　*　　　*

Since then I have caught every kind of freshwater fish, but I can remember only one other first: my first salmon.

John initiated me into spinning and fly fishing for trout later that summer. By autumn I was eager for a salmon, but John told me to be patient and wait until the next year's spring run.

'Too close to spawning, a lot of 'em,' he said. 'Your first salmon should be a clean fish.'

So, one evening early in March, came a 'phone call from John.

'When are you free this week, Bob?'

'I've a surgery tomorrow morning, but I'm clear in the afternoon.'

'Couldn't be better. Try to get to the cottage about half past one. Might be able to put you in touch with a salmon. Don't worry about the gear. Right?'

'Right.'

John was waiting outside the cottage when I arrived, a rod already assembled and baited with a spinner, a metal lure with vanes which revolved round a central pivot, and armed with a wicked treble hook.

'Right, Bob,' he said. 'We won't hang about. The run's well under way now, and there's one feller I've had my eye on since yesterday. He's been jumping about cleaning off his sea lice, and he's been resting up in the narrow pool below the bridge. He won't stay there much longer, though, so we'd better go and say hello.'

'Thank you very much, John,' I said, eyeing the nine-and-a-half-foot rod with what must have been ill-disguised disappointment. 'Will this rod be big enough to hold him?'

'Oh, yes, Cleverclogs,' he said. 'You've been watching them show-offs with the twelve-footers. Well take no notice. This rod's plenty long enough – and if this feller takes you past those trees on the bank you'll be damn glad you've only got nine feet of it to worry about.'

The salmon was lying deep, in the middle of the pool and facing upstream. I could just about see the dark shape, with the occasional glint of silver, in the spot where John was pointing.

'Right,' said John. 'Cast upstream, and bring the spinner back across his nose and past him. More than likely he won't budge for the first few goes, but then he'll get annoyed. Go on, lad – get stuck in.'

Spinning back downstream can be tricky, because you have to reel in faster than the current to get any movement in the spinner and to stop it sinking right to the bottom and possibly getting snagged. But I managed it, once, twice, three times, bringing the lure towards the salmon – or at least towards where the salmon was lying, because it was impossible to concentrate on the lure and see the fish at the same time.

Four times . . . five and – bang! The line tautened and the rod tip bent like a bow.

'Got him!' shouted John. 'Strike again for luck.' (I hadn't actually struck – the salmon had done it for me – but I knew what John meant.)

I struck into what felt like a rock. There was a pause.

'Keep the line taut, but be ready to give some!' shouted John.

Then the rock moved, shunting upstream at a speed which had the line running out from the reel at a frightening rate. Then it stopped.

'Take in the slack,' shouted John. 'Keep contact. And be ready for him to turn.'

Turn it did, charging downstream towards me this time, making me crank like mad to take up the slack line. The fish went downstream past me, with the current to help its bulk, and I just managed to turn its head before it reached the broken water at the tail of the pool.

Up and down and across the fish went, with the danger of a broken line at every turn, every shake of its head. Three or four times it leapt clear of the water, and I remembered John's instructions to drop the rod tip as the fish fell back. I was really glad to be in charge of only a nine-and-a-half-foot rod. A twelve-footer would have been bound to hit the trees on the bank above me.

The fight seemed to last for hours. My arms were aching from playing the fish, my eyes aching from straining to see the line where it cut the water in an attempt to forecast the fish's next move.

'How long does this go on for?' I yelled.

John looked at his watch.

'I reckon it's a fifteen-pounder,' he said, 'and you can usually reckon on a minute to the pound. Won't be long now.'

After a couple of minutes he shouted, 'Come in, number fifteen – your time's up!' and stepped into the shallow water by the bank with a tailer, a wire noose on a short handle.

He was right. By now the fish was fairly beaten, and I was able to manoeuvre it upstream towards John.

A dip with the tailer, a double-handed snatch – and there was this beautiful, yard-long, streamlined silver creature thrashing on the bank.

John knelt on it swiftly and with a 'clunk' administered the *coup de grâce* with one blow of the priest.

I staggered over, my arms shaking and my knees like jelly. Proud as I was, a dreadful sense of anti-climax set in.

'It's so beautiful,' I said. 'Seems a pity it's . . . it's . . .'

'Dead?' said John.

'Yes.'

'Much better that way, lad. Otherwise you'd have a hell of a job keeping the bugger in the oven . . .'

6

The Little People

Living in the Tadchester area were several characters who were so small in size that it made me sometimes wonder whether there was once a race of small people in Somerset.

Whether or not it was some aboriginal strain in the local ethnic mixture, whether there really was once a race of tiny folk in Somerset, I don't know, but there certainly were several very, very small people among the inhabitants. They weren't dwarfs and didn't appear to have been stunted by any dietary defects. They were just perfectly formed tiny folk.

The first two I met really gave me the willies. I called at a cottage right off the beaten track. A beautiful place with a well-tended little garden, a yellow-tiled roof and wistaria growing up the side and spreading across under the eaves.

Beautiful as it was, there was something strange about it. When the door was opened I found myself saying 'Good evening' to empty air, and was answered by a voice which came from somewhere just below my waist. It was a tiny, very tiny, old lady, wrinkled like a dried apple. She was very old but spotlessly dressed in an old-fashioned long frock and apron, with bright and very brown eyes.

'Oh,' I said, recovering myself. 'I'm Dr Clifford. I've called to see Mr Fletcher. Am I speaking to Mrs Fletcher?'

'That's right, Doctor,' she said in a thin piping voice. 'Do come in.'

Sitting by the fire in the living room with a shawl around his shoulders was a little old man. A tiny old man. When he stood up to greet me he was about an inch taller than the tiny old lady.

The room was full of normal-sized furniture but it looked giant-sized against the elfin frames of the two old people. It was really eerie to see them moving about amongst enormous chairs, an enormous table, and an enormous grandfather clock which filled the room with its loud tick and rattled the teacups with its chime.

Strangest of all, however, was the creature which sat opposite the old man in front of the fire. It was a cat, but the biggest cat I had ever seen. Almost like a tiger. A yellow creature that watched me through enormous and luminous slanting green eyes as I examined the old man's chest.

'How old are you Mr Fletcher?' I asked.

'Eighty-one,' he replied in the same fluting voice as the old lady.

'He's eighty-one,' echoed the old lady, proudly.

'And you are looking well on it,' I said. 'Nothing wrong with you, Mr Fletcher, that keeping warm and dry won't put right. I'll give you a prescription for some linctus to help clear your chest. Take a tablespoonful three times a day.'

The old man nodded.

'You'll make sure your husband takes it won't you Mrs Fletcher?' I said.

'He's not my husband,' piped the old lady. 'He's my son.'

The grandfather clock whirred and struck the hour with a resonance which by rights should have shaken the windows out.

Eighty-one and her son! I must leave, I thought, before I turn into a pumpkin.

I took one last glance behind as the old lady closed the door. In front of the fire still sat the enormous yellow cat, grinning at me. The Cheshire cat was alive and well in deepest Somerset!

As I fastened the garden gate in the neat and freshly painted white fence, I realised what was odd about the cottage. It was the Gingerbread House! I drove back to Tadchester as quickly as I could and downed a large scotch in the Tadchester Arms. Imagination, I told myself, nothing more. But I still shiver every time I think about the little cottage, with two tiny people and the enormous yellow cat . . .

*   *   *

Another tiny person I treated was Ranger, the cowman. Nobody knew Ranger's other name, not even Ranger. He had no birth certificate and didn't know how old he was. With his permission I entered him on the records as John Ranger, but all he had ever been was Ranger, and had been for as long as even the old-timers could remember.

I was talking to Kevin Bird in the Tadchester Market one day – Kevin conducted most of the cattle auctions there – when we were interrupted by Josh Palmer, a local farmer. Palmer had a superb dairy herd and was reputed to have a lot of money, which he was also reputed to be very loath to part with. He came up and said, 'You the doctor?'

'One of them, yes,' I said, taking an instant dislike to him. 'My name's Clifford.'

'You'll do,' said Palmer. 'Better come down tomorrow and look at Ranger. He's took badly. Coughing all over the place. Can't have that when there's milk about. Dozy little tyke, can't hardly get out in the morning, either.'

'Who's Ranger?' I asked.

'I thought everybody knew that. Me cowman. Little feller. Lives in the bottom field behind me farm. Fourways Farm, over towards Winchcombe.'

'I'll call in the morning.'

'Right. See you do.'

'Look here,' I started, intending to give a short, sharp homily on manners. But Palmer had abruptly turned his back and walked away out of the market.

'Don't let him upset you Bob,' said Kevin. 'He's always like that: even worse on market days when he has to sell some of his milked-out cows. I'm just off to see what I can do for him. Take care. We hope you and Pam will come round at the weekend and have something to eat.'

As I turned to go I bumped into John Denton the River Authority bailiff.

'Hey up, our Bob,' he said in his broad Manchester accent. 'You look as if you've swallowed a quid and found a tanner. What's the matter?'

'Nothing, John. I've just had the pleasure of meeting Josh Palmer.'

'Him? Miserable old bugger. Wouldn't give you the snot from his nose. What's he been up to?'

I explained and asked John about Ranger and where exactly he lived.

'Poor little feller,' said John. 'A nice enough lad, but not the full shilling. Lad! He's more like a bloody gernommy. Tiny little bloke he is, Palmer's cowman. Knee-high to a shit bucket. He can do anything with them cows, bulls an' all.

'He saved Palmer's life one day when that big bull of his pinned the old sod to the shippon wall. Just walked under its nose, got hold of the ring in his little hand, stood on tip-toe and sang into its ear. Bloody *sang*, at a time like that. Any road, it worked. The old bull calmed down and walked back with Ranger to the stall quiet as a lamb.

'Palmer was all right, apart from a couple of cracked ribs, and for once in his life he dug into his pocket. Raised Ranger's wages he did, on the spot. Just as well – given time he'd have thought better of it.'

'That's something in Palmer's favour anyway,' I said. 'What did he raise them to?'

'Seven and six a week.'

'What? What was he getting before?'

'Seven shillings.'

'John, you're kidding.'

'There's plenty in here will tell you the same,' said John. 'Bloody slave labour that little fellow is, and he's worth three ordinary cowmen. But, as I said, he's not full muster. Got a screw loose somewhere and he's grateful to Palmer for giving him a roof. Scared he'll lose it if he upsets the old bugger.'

'What is the roof John?' I asked, 'So that I'll know what to look for tomorrow. A cottage?'

'Cottage?' shrieked John, as he fell about laughing. Then he shouted across to some of his cronies having a cup of tea and a bun at the mobile tea stand. 'Ranger! Doc's on about Ranger. Wants to know if he lives in a cottage!'

The cronies and everyone else within earshot fell about laughing, and John bellowed above the din, 'Cottage be buggered! The poor little sod lives in the back of a lorry!'

Backward and feudal as some parts of Somerset were, I just couldn't believe that a man could be kept in conditions worse than those of the animals he tended, and paid a pittance which would scarcely feed a dog for a week.

The next morning I discovered that it was true. In the bottom of the field behind Fourways Farm stood an old lorry, wheelless and jacked up on four piles of stones. The back of it was covered by a tarpaulin. Inside I found Ranger.

What looked like the body of a seven-year-old child lay on a pile of sacks, covered by some more sacking. The face was obviously that of an elderly man but it had the strangely young look of the simple minded. From the tiny body came staccato bursts of coughing, and wheezing attempts to suck air into the lungs.

A very brief examination was enough. Ranger had pneumonia and pleurisy. I said, 'Ranger, you need somewhere drier and warmer than this if you are going to get better. I will arrange a ride to hospital for you. You will have a nice warm bed and nice kind nurses to look after you.'

'No, no!' wheezed the little man. 'My cows! My cows! Who'll look after my cows?'

'Mr Palmer will look after them while you are away, Ranger. And it won't be for long. If you stay like this you will make the cows poorly, and you wouldn't like that would you?'

'No. But what about my home? It'll be here when I get back won't it? Master won't let anybody else live here will he?'

'No, Ranger,' I said, looking around at the clammy tarpaulin which constituted the walls of the home. 'He certainly won't. I'll see to that.'

I drove back to the nearest telephone box and arranged for an ambulance to take Ranger to the Tadchester hospital. I didn't want to ask for the use of Palmer's phone, assuming he had one. Ranger must be got away quickly out of the old villain's clutches. He was taken to hospital just in time: another twenty-four hours and he would have been filling a very small coffin.

As it was, he made steady but good progress. I saw him most days in the ward in the hospital. He was a great favourite with the Sister and the staff. John Bowler, the physician from Winchcombe who came over from time to time, cast a specialist eye on him and took some fluid from his chest which speeded his recovery. It was not long before he was out and about walking round the ward, pushing the tea trolley, and being treated as benevolently by the other men in the ward as if he were a little boy. He loved hospital – he never conceived that life could be as pleasant, as warm, and as comfortable as this – but he still hankered after his cows.

In the meantime I had not been idle on his behalf. What I

should say is that others had not been idle. I put the word out to a few chosen friends like John Denton, Kevin Bird and Joe Church. Ranger would be far better off with another job, a decent roof over his head and a living, if modest, wage. Within two days there were offers of jobs from four farmers, two with cottages thrown in. This was not generosity on their part: Ranger had the reputation of being the best cowman for miles around.

Ranger took a great deal of persuading. He was terrified of Palmer and dreaded some revenge, not to mention being almost grief-stricken at the thought of parting from his beloved cows.

Mrs Bemrose, the local social worker, talked gently to Ranger for some hours spread over several days. She assured him that Palmer was powerless to take any action against him. She drummed into him all the benefits of the jobs which were offered. She made him realise that he would be paid money he found hard even to imagine, and finally gave the little man some sense of his own worth. Ranger accepted a job with the farmer whose herd most closely resembled Palmer's, and there was a snug little cottage to go with the job.

Mrs Bemrose acted swiftly, getting an order from the Council Health Department declaring the lorry unfit for human habitation, so that Palmer could not enslave another poor soul as he had done Ranger. She also contacted the local Rotary Club who stocked the cottage up with secondhand but serviceable furniture, and by the time Ranger was discharged from hospital he had a fully equipped home to go to. It was beyond his wildest dreams.

I drove Ranger home from hospital to the cottage myself. The farmer's wife had a hot meal waiting for him. The farmer, a gruff but kindly man, greeted him warmly.

'When you're fit, Ranger,' he said, 'I'll show you round the farm and you can get to know the stock. But there's no hurry. Get fit first and let me know when you would like to start.'

'I've got my boots on, Master,' said Ranger, pointing to the child-sized wellingtons on his spindly legs. 'If it's all right with you, I'll just finish this food first.'

From then on Ranger never looked back. The farmer got more than his money's worth out of him. The dairy and the shippon (cowhouse) were always spotless, the milk yield increased and sickness amongst the herd dropped almost to nothing.

For the first time in his life Ranger had a home which was warm and dry, and he kept it scrubbed and tidy. The little man had come into his own. But not before time . . . and no more than he deserved.

7

Pregnant Moments

Hovery was the most famous beauty spot in the whole area. It was a village which lay at the foot of the cliffs and which could only be approached by a very steep, pebbly road. The road wound in and out through cottages and you thought, as you walked down it, that at each corner you would reach the bottom. When you eventually did reach the bottom, you found you'd walked much further than you originally intended. For some of the older holidaymakers it was too much, and every year we had several coronaries among the people attempting to walk back up the Hovery hill.

At one time supplies were taken down to the harbour by donkey or sledge. It wasn't until later years that another track parallel to the main village street was hacked out along the cliff face, enabling a Landrover to ferry supplies and some of the less fit holidaymakers.

Hovery was really out of the practice area, but one or two patients still hung on and demanded our services as they did in Dratchet.

In days gone by, the Hovery people had lived in a small, inbred community and had a high incidence of mentally retarded children. Mongolism was very common in and around the area. I had a great affection for the mongols, those sweet, gentle children who would never grow up and who never became aggressive. Whenever I was called to Hovery there would always be several of them scampering around trying to help carry my bag.

Many of the farms around Hovery assimilated a mongol child, whether their own or somebody else's, into the family. The children helped with small tasks round the farm. Some could milk the cows, chop wood, and do other simple jobs, and they added a useful complement to the families that had taken them in. The very location of the farms on which they lived protected them from the more sophisticated society outside where they would have found it difficult to cope.

*　　　*　　　*

Two new friends who had joined our circle in Tadchester – Philip and Joan Gammon – bought a cottage on the Hovery road, about five miles out of Tadchester itself.

Philip had taken up a post as games and physical education master at Tadchester Boys' Grammar School, and Joan taught the same subjects at Tadchester Girls' Grammar School. Philip had taken the place of Joe Church, one of our closest friends, who'd gone off to join the Royal Air Force. We missed Joe and his wife Lee, but Philip and Joan couldn't have been better replacements.

Philip was a keen naturalist. He had a couple of acres of ground around his cottage and started a sanctuary for birds of prey. He became an expert – one of the few in the whole country – on the care and keeping of these birds. Sick and injured birds from all over were brought for his medical care. On two or three occasions, with a little help from me, he even got birds x-rayed at Tadchester Hospital.

Philip and Joan had been living in their cottage for about a year when Joan became pregnant. It was her first pregnancy and it was taken for granted that I would look after her, as I looked after and delivered the babies of all my friends. Although I was pleased to do it, and would have been offended if I hadn't been asked, it was always more of a strain looking after people with whom you were friendly, related, or close in any way. The very nature of the relationship was such that it wasn't quite so easy to make clear, or anyway dispassionate, judgments.

Happily, Joan had no trouble with her pregnancy at all. She was very fit, she was pleasant natured and easy going, and the confinement was to take place in the small bedroom up the sharply winding stairs of their cottage.

As she was a friend I gave her all those little bits of extra attention. I took her blood pressure a bit more often, tested her water a bit more often, and kept a closer watch generally like the fussy old hen that I was always accused of being. Nurse Plank was to be the attending midwife. It was always a great comfort to me when she was there: she did all the work and I was happy just to obey her instructions.

All seemed set for a happy and straightforward delivery. I called round to see Joan on a Wednesday evening, checked her blood pressure, and checked that her water was clear. She felt fine, but was beginning to get twinges of pain.

'I think this is it, Joan,' I said. 'I have the feeling you are going to give me a disturbed night.'

At three o'clock in the morning there was a call from Philip. I arrived there just in time to pretend to assist Nurse Plank in the very straightforward delivery of an eight-pound girl. I was pleased to get the birth over because I did tend to worry about pregnancies. All was absolutely fine. Mother fine, baby fine, after a successful confinement at home. This was just how childbirth should be.

I was back home by eight o'clock to tell Pam the news, and we were almost as pleased as they were. Pam called in to see Joan during the morning and took her some flowers. Philip was busy writing out funny cards to announce the birth of the child.

At two o'clock in the afternoon as I was starting surgery, Gladys came racing in.

'Quick! they want you urgently at the Gammons'.'

Gladys never panicked unnecessarily. When she said you had to go quickly, then there was no doubt it was urgent.

Gladys was one of the best sifters of cases that I ever met. She could distinguish the important cases very clearly from the ones that were less so.

Obviously something was wrong. Phil was a very level-headed person, not a panicker, and a message like this meant that something pretty awful must have happened.

As I drove as fast as I could up the Hovery road to their cottage I permutated all the things that could be happening to Joan. I thought that she could be bleeding or had something worse, like a cerebral haemorrhage. Or the baby could have choked.

I broke all personal speed records in getting to the cottage. I raced up the stairs, and there was Joan in bed, unconscious, grey in the face, and looking desperately ill.

'Oh my God,' I thought. 'She's had a cerebral haemorrhage.'

Joan suddenly started to twitch and went into a fit. She needed an injection before she eventually stopped convulsing.

Phil was almost as ashen as Joan. I sent him off to phone for an ambulance and just sat there by the bed, counting the minutes until the ambulance arrived. Joan's condition didn't change much. She looked grey, her lips looked blue, her face looked swollen and her breathing was stertorous. The baby was fine, crying lustily from its cot in the corner.

At last the ambulance arrived. We then had to get Joan down the stairs. The local ambulance men had a kind of canvas sling that we slid under Joan to carry her downstairs like a parcel. The winding stairs of the cottage, which had always seemed fun and full of character, now presented terrible problems. We at last got Joan, still unconscious, into the ambulance and it rushed off to the maternity unit at Winchcombe.

Although the couple were by now my closest of friends, I breathed a sigh of relief that the responsibility of looking after Joan would be in somebody else's hands. The maternity unit at Winchcombe hospital was new, and I knew that Joan would have the best possible care.

I just could not think what could be wrong. I'd never had any situation like this before, and I still had a terrible fear that Joan had a brain haemorrhage, though it was a rare occurrence in young people.

It also looked a bit like a pregnancy fit. One of the main reasons an expectant mother attended a doctor in those days was to see that the blood pressure didn't come up, and that there was no protein in the urine. These were signs of what was called toxaemia of pregnancy, which might progress into an eclamptic fit. Such a fit was a great worry before midwifery became more sophisticated, and better drugs became available.

But Joan's condition had come about *after* the baby was born. I'd checked both urine and blood pressure only the night before and they were perfectly normal.

I rang the hospital later in the day and was told that Joan had what they called a *post-partum* eclamptic fit. This meant that she had a fit related to pregnancy, but *after* the birth of the child. I didn't even know that this could happen.

I came back to the surgery and made for the great tomes on midwifery in Steve Maxwell's room. I pored through them and eventually, in one American volume, I read that there had been a few reported cases of *post-partum* eclamptic fits. I took it as a reflection on my learning.

In my early days of practice at Tadchester, any doctor you met would tell you horrifying tales of ladies with toxaemia of pregnancy lying dangerously ill in darkened rooms, away from any noise that might start them off in a fit. Once the baby had been born and removed from the mother the toxaemia of pregnancy finished. It was thought that it was some sort of mother's allergy to her own baby. It was a rare condition before baby was born. It was a very, very rare condition *after* baby was born. Trust one of my friends to produce it, I thought.

Joan had a stormy time, was unconscious for a couple of days, but in a week was fully recovered, full of beans, home with a healthy baby and with a guarantee that there would be no after effects. It was a tremendous relief to see her home and well again.

*   *   *

I had been anxious for Joan's confinement to be on time for an ulterior motive. Kevin Bird, Janice, Pam and I had booked a cabin cruiser at Oxford for a week's holiday on the Thames. I couldn't have gone if Joan had been late, or hadn't recovered from her illness so soon.

We'd all been rather hard pressed at the practice and I badly needed a holiday. We called in to see Joan before we left. She was her old natural self, sitting up talking animatedly. It was with great relief that we packed up our car with Janice and Kevin and motored off to Oxford to pick up our cabin cruiser at Folly Bridge.

I love the Thames. As a schoolboy, I and a group of friends used to hire camping rowing boats. Five or six of us would pile into one of these boats and tear away downriver, trying to break all rowing records during the day. At night we would spread canvas over the special hoops on the boat, roll out mattresses, and sleep in the bottom. It was a bit like a floating covered wagon. We'd do our cooking on the bank, and we had the river to wash in.

It was really all good boy scout stuff, and I loved every minute of it. I vowed that one day I'd do it in comfort in a cabin cruiser where there were such sophisticated things as lights, a cooking stove and somewhere to wash.

So this was to be our holiday. We pulled in to our car park just by Folly Bridge to find our craft moored at the bottom of some steps by the bridge. It looked, to put it kindly, a little bit dilapidated. There were lots of superb looking craft around. Ours was by far the oldest and most battered. We immediately called her the *African Queen*.

'I'll be Humphrey Bogart,' I said to Pam, 'and you can be Katharine Hepburn.'

The holiday with Janice and Kevin was in very early May and we'd brought along plenty of warm clothes with us. Janice in particular had boxes, cases, coats, even a fur coat. We had to unload these from the car, deposit them on the towpath and then drive the car off to park it in the boatyard.

Our stuff on the towpath – huge mounds of cardboard boxes

and various items of clothing, particularly Janice's – almost blocked the right of way. The college eights were coming down to row and they were terribly amused to see this great pile of equipment, enough for a good-sized safari. They launched their boats by the side of us, and offered to take the girls with them for nothing.

Somehow we got everything aboard and packed after a fashion. The next problem was how to turn round in the cabins. There were two two-berth cabins, with bunks either side of a central gangway. There was a small stove and sink at one end and a large Calor gas cylinder perched on the back of the boat. A battery was charged from the engine and there was electric light, or so we were told.

Having loaded up, we went back to make our final checks with the boat office and to pick up maps of the river. There was an urgent OHMS envelope waiting for us.

My heart sank. We both so needed a holiday, particularly after the strain of Joan's baby. Could this mysterious envelope contain something to spoil it?

I opened it. Out came a long sheet of printed paper which I couldn't understand at first. Then the penny dropped: it was a notice of prosecution for taking underweight fish out of the sea.

We used to trawl the beaches at Sanford-on-Sea with a seine net and never queried the size of the mesh, which was the same as the commercial fishermen used. All of us shared the net – Janice, Kevin, Eric, Zara, Joan and Philip. Why suddenly pick on me? And how had they found me at Oxford? I was a bit worried because I had twice taken some sea trout out of the sea, but to my knowledge I had never taken undersized fish.

Pam could see I was worried and said, 'Oh, darling, surely it can't be bad news? Not just as we're starting this holiday?'

I turned the notice over. There was a funny drawing of a man and his wife and a tiny baby. Written underneath it was, 'Have a good holiday, and just leave those little tiddlers be – Philip and Joan.'

'The wretch!' I thought, laughing with relief. 'Just wait till I get back home.'

We pushed off from Oxford with the boat laden almost to the gunwales. It was cold and there was a slight drizzle. We were glad that we had all our warm clothes with us. The forecast was that the weather was going to be even colder still.

We only went a few hundred yards downriver on our first night. We practised circling the boat and getting used to all the problems of stopping, starting, and turning it round. We moored at the side of the bank, went to a pub for dinner, and came back into this cold, smelly boat. We put all our clothes on to keep us warm – and woke up sweating in the morning to find the sun blazing down on us. The sun shone for a whole week. All the mass of clothing that we had brought with us stayed where it was until the holiday was over.

I had brought a pair of rugby shorts with me just in case the weather improved. These and a pair of gym shoes were all I wore. I'd also tucked away a pair of legged bathing trunks. Kevin borrowed these and used them as shorts. The girls had light clothes and Janice had a very revealing bathing costume.

These were virtually the only clothes we wore for the whole week.

Our boat truly lived up to the name *African Queen*. It seemed to break down almost every other mile along the river. We somehow managed to struggle down to Abingdon, Goring, Pangbourne and Sonning. Each time we broke down, some fresh new mechanic from the boat company would appear, take one look at the boat, say 'Good God! Is this thing still running?'

Although they were a terrible nuisance, our stops, the cups of tea and the laughs we had with various mechanics all seemed part of the holiday. The enforced stops made us spend a longer time in areas that we would not normally have given much time.

Pam's parents came up from Leatherhead and met us at the Swan at Goring for lunch. At Abingdon we had dinner with Joe Church and his wife. Joe was posted there to the RAF Parachute Training School. We took them for a trip down the river after dinner.

None of us was very nautical. Kevin and I took it in turns to take the wheel and we used the girls as slaves to jump out and moor us tight into the bank as we went through locks.

Only once did the girls each have a go at steering. Pam insisted on taking us in to the Swan at Goring. Heedless of our advice she approached the quay going at full tilt. She meant, she said later, to put the brake on when she got there. She hit the jetty with such a whack I am sure she pushed the hotel back three or four feet.

Janice decided to do her steering along a canal lock. She got distracted and started to head for the bank. Some workmen sitting on the side eating their lunch saw the boat approaching at speed, dropped their sandwiches and ran up the bank. It was the only time I have seen men chased by a boat. Kevin and I were almost helpless with laughter. Janice got us lodged half way up the bank. It took all our efforts and those of the workmen – whose panic was now over – to get us afloat again.

The crazy incidents were just part of the whole delightful week. With the unexpected brilliant sunshine, the uncrowded river, the plentiful wildlife, it was often enough to sit and watch the world go by.

It was marvellous to wake up in the morning and sit in the cockpit of the boat, with bacon and eggs frying, surrounded by swans. Then in the daytime, to wander slowly through the locks and explore the riverside towns. Henley, Wallingford, Maidenhead and Marlow . . . they each have their special memories now.

Pam had brought with her Jerome K. Jerome's *Three Men in a Boat*, and we went to many of the places his characters had visited.

Too soon, as with all good things, the holiday was over and we were on our way back to Tadchester, fit and bronzed, with a whole heap of unused luggage. We said goodbye to our boat, which now sat forlornly on the side of the quay. We'd cursed it and sworn at it, but in the end had got very attached to it. I think it was probably the boat's swansong. It was so decrepit that it could not have stayed afloat much longer: we must have been pretty well the last people to use it. Over the years we had many river holidays, but never ever caught sight of it again. At least I can say now, when the conversation turns to boats, 'Yes – reminds me of the time I was aboard the *African Queen* . . .'

8

Happy Families

Soon after returning from our river holiday with Kevin and Janice, I began to worry about Pam's health. Her appetite began to fall away and she was not at all interested in going out.

She had always been prone to car sickness but now she was sick even on short journeys, and once or twice I found that she'd been sick and hadn't told me.

It is very difficult as a doctor to treat your own family and I imagined a whole lot of fearsome conditions. It must be cancer or tuberculosis or something like that: it wouldn't be anything simple, I was sure.

Pam refused to go and see Steve Maxwell, saying 'I'm sure it will pass. I'll work it off.' However, a couple of weeks went by and she didn't work it off. She felt awful particularly in the mornings, was hardly eating at all, and was gradually losing weight.

I'd promised not to mention her illness to my partners but now, realising how poorly she was getting, she reluctantly agreed to let Steve Maxwell see her. Steve was round in an hour. I realised why his patients were so devoted to him: just to have him in the house was a great comfort. As soon as he had opened the door, I knew that everything was going to be all right.

He went up to the bedroom where he examined Pam and listened to her history, then came down to me. He had a half smile on his face which I thought was unlike him when a patient, especially Pam, was so obviously ill.

'Before making a complete diagnosis we'd better just check Pam's water,' he said, 'but I don't think it's too much to worry about.'

How often had I said this to patients before, thinking I was reassuring them? If Steve said it wasn't too much to worry about, it probably meant that there *was* something to worry about, and I was one of the world's greatest worriers.

It took two days for the test on Pam's urine to come back, and Steve called me in to his surgery that morning. I was full of anxiety when I went in.

'My diagnosis is confirmed,' he said, 'and I'm surprised that a bright young medical rising star like you didn't think of it straight away.

'Pam's condition is quite curable. I don't know quite how long her symptoms are going to continue, particularly her sickness. But from my estimation, in about seven months' time she will be completely cured of anything to do with this particular problem – although she might have new responsibilities and extra things to take care of.'

It didn't strike me for a minute what he was trying to tell me, and then I realised – Pam was pregnant. Whereas with every woman patient of childbearing age I would have thought of it straight away, I had missed the obvious when it came to looking after my own wife.

Pam took it all in her stride after her initial sickness, which ended after about twelve weeks. She went her full nine months and went conveniently into labour one Saturday afternoon when I was off duty. I took her over to Winchcombe and she was delivered by lunchtime the next day.

Steve had thought it not a good idea for her to be looked after by one of the partners. He said, 'It's so difficult when you are making medical decisions about people you know very well, particularly people whom you work with. Your judgment can be impaired by the emotional involvement.' Happily, as everything turned out, no judgments were really called for.

I was having lunch with Kevin and Janice, and our old friends Frank and Primrose, when we heard the news that Pam had given birth to a seven and a half-pound boy. We dashed over to Winchcombe and there was Pam looking as if she had been a mother all her life, with a sort of horrible pink bawling thing – Trevor – nestling in the crook of her arm.

Life changed when Trevor came home. I had to get used to damp nappies and interrupted nights, but we fared better than most. Trevor was one of the most docile, placid and self-contained babies I had ever met. As he grew older we would put him in his play pen and he was perfectly content to sit and watch the world go by.

When Trevor was three years old, Pam began again to have the symptoms of sickness and loss of appetite. This time I was able to make the diagnosis without calling for a second opinion – Pam was pregnant again.

Whereas her pregnancy with Trevor had been smooth, with this pregnancy she had all sorts of upsets. There was a false alarm that she was going to go into labour early. The date on which she was expecting to be delivered came and went. Another week passed, and then a second week, and we were beginning to despair.

On my Sunday off, we took the car out and went for a ride along one of the bumpiest tracks we could find in the practice – and by two o'clock the next morning Pam had started in labour.

We had nobody to leave Trevor with, so we wrapped him up in the back of the car for the ten-mile drive to Winchcombe. The atmosphere in the car was tense: Pam was gritting her teeth through the contractions, and I was hunched, grim-faced, over the steering wheel. There was a strained silence which was suddenly broken by the piping voice of Trevor saying, 'We haven't had swede for lunch lately, have we?'

At this, Pam and I both roared with laughter. It took away all the tension and the worry of getting her to hospital in time. We toyed with the idea of calling the new arrival 'Swede', but we didn't think we'd get away with it.

We arrived at the hospital at five o'clock in the morning, and

were met by a grumpy, breathless midwife who examined Pam while I waited.

'You doctors are all the same,' the midwife said to me after the examination. 'Rushing in with your wives before they have started in labour. She'll be hours yet – she hasn't even begun. The best thing *you* can do is go home.'

Crestfallen, I took Trevor back home. I couldn't go to sleep. At quarter past six the phone rang and the grumpy midwife was on the line.

'What's the matter?' I said, alarmed, thinking that at the very least she was ringing me to tell me to bring Pam home again.

'You've got another boy,' she said.

'You told me she wasn't in labour,' I said.

'Oh, the enema I gave her brought it on,' said Mrs Grumpy, determined not to be caught out.

And so Paul was born.

* * *

Of all the things in my life, I cannot think of anything more important, or which has given me more pleasure, than my children. Pam and I have been lucky that the children have always got on well together and always been extremely fond of each other. Trevor welcomed his new little brother home joyfully. He was going through the three-year-old's passion for hats – almost a fetish – and spent many happy hours putting hats on the new arrival. A baby brother was a live, moveable object on which he could place any one of his collection of hats and admire them from his customary Buddha-like position.

Whereas Trevor had been quiet and docile, Paul was noisy. He had us awake at night, worried the life out of us, and was completely different in nature. Though they were so different, they were complementary. Trevor was hard-working, devoured books, and read anything he could lay his hands on from the earliest age. Paul was about as unacademic as it is possible to be, never read anything and lived in a world of dreams with a virile imagination. Strangely, he was always meticulous in the care of the equipment of whichever sport in which he was going to represent England at the time, whether it was cricket, hockey, or football.

Having children of my own gave me a much greater depth of understanding of the problems that women had with their babies, and the problems of the babies themselves. Before I became a father, I had nonchalantly advised mothers how to cope with a baby who cried at night, a baby who was constipated, a baby who wouldn't take its food. Dealing with my own children was another problem altogether, and I was always asking Nurse Plank what was the right thing to do.

Nurse Plank had taken care of Pam and both boys as soon as they had come home from hospital. She was an absolute godsend. I wished I could have kept her in the house. Despite all my experience and my supposed knowledge, if either of the babies wasn't crying I was always poking in the cot to see if they had stopped breathing. If either *was* crying, I was always rushing in to see if anything was wrong.

Pam had made friends with a widow, Margaret Buck, and her daughter Sally. Sally was about four years older than Trevor and behaved like an elder sister towards both boys. Over the years, Margaret and Sally became part of the family. Margaret, the ever-generous, came on many family holidays with us. We used to pull her leg about her habit of walking round with her handbag open, eager to pay for everything that was going.

Just a few months after Paul was born, Zara, Pam's other close friend, had her first baby, Nicholas. The extrovert Zara had had a quiet wedding. Whether she had been put off by our wedding, or the fact that it was her dress design that led to the bridesmaids' see-through dresses, I don't know, but she abandoned all ideas of a large wedding of her own. She had threatened Eric with all sorts of fancy weddings, including one at which he'd have to wear a white suit and a white top hat, but one day they just slipped off on their own to a register office and came back married.

*   *   *

Pam and I went through most of the heartbreaks that other parents experience on seeing their children first go off to school. From the back window of our house we could just see to the yard of the primary school, which lay to one side of Fred Derrigan's smallholding. On Trevor's first day I caught Pam at the bedroom window with tears streaming down her cheeks.

We both looked together into the school yard and there was a group of boys playing. Standing on the outside hopping on one foot, wanting to join them but not knowing how to, was Trevor, all on his own.

'Come away, darling,' I said. 'He'll settle in in no time' – trying to hide the fact that I was feeling very choked up myself.

The first day at school of one's first child is so traumatic. In the past I'd reassured mothers and patted them comfortingly on the head, not understanding why they were getting upset. The children were just going off for the day and they'd be back in the evening. Having it happen to one's own children was a very, very different proposition. Although I'd always examined children with care, I examined them with even more care once I had children of my own.

*   *   *

When Paul was quite young, Pam decided to resume her amateur stage activities. On one of the first dates we ever had, I had to go and see her performing as a maid with the Fetcham Players, a company from near Leatherhead, very much on a par with the Tadchester Drama Society.

Pam would pop off two or three nights a week to rehearsals in Tadchester. She would get my evening meal ready and leave it in the oven if I wasn't back in time. I was quite happy about it all and glad she was taking part in the town's activities. Apparently her experience in Fetcham counted very highly in Tadchester and she was to play the lead in the next production. Things went well until four weeks before the opening night, when Pam came down to breakfast feeling poorly. There were two large tell-tale swellings behind her ears.

'Look Bob – whatever's happened to me? Am I allergic to something?'

'No,' I said. 'I'm afraid you've got mumps – you ought to be ashamed of yourself.'

Sometimes infectious diseases play strange tricks. Among the young mothers in Tadchester that year there was an epidemic of mumps. Although Paul and Trevor were often in bed with Pam in the early morning, and I am sure many of the other children at Trevor's school were in their mothers' beds, none of the children caught mumps. But many of the adults did, and they were very poorly with it.

So Pam, with her stage production looming, was confined to the house and feeling very ill. Margaret Buck came over to help as often as she could, despite the fact that she was frightened of catching mumps herself.

'How long will I take to get better?' Pam kept on asking, worried at the prospect of letting the whole drama company down.

I didn't look after her myself, but left it in the hands of Steve Maxwell. After two weeks, he allowed Pam to get up, but not to go out. With the production now only a fortnight away, the Society was desperate, so it was decided that rehearsals would be held in our lounge. We had quite a large lounge which opened on to a dining room, separated by a huge hanging curtain. Although it didn't make an ideal setting, the players could rehearse and make a show of drawing the curtain back and presenting their play.

Herbert Barlow, who always swore that he wouldn't have anything to do with amateurs, came along and helped them with their direction and lines and advised them about scenery.

Steve said Pam would be fit enough to leave the house and actually appear in the play the following week, but she would have to continue rehearsing at home almost to the last minute.

With rehearsals going every night for two weeks, I had to fend for myself when I came in in the evening. The house was full of strangers. I would go into the kitchen and find the odd person lifting the lid of the pan in which I was trying to cook a meal, just to check what I was having for dinner.

I breathed a sigh of relief when at last the drama society left the house. I had Pam to myself for a whole Sunday – and then she disappeared for a whole week, appearing first at the Tadchester Hall and then at the Plaza Cinema, Winchcombe.

I went over on the last night with Gerry and Bill, Pam's father and mother, who were looking at houses in the area and staying in Winchcombe. I had to watch Pam embraced, a bit too lovingly I thought, by her leading man who I recognised as a bearded clerk from the Surveyor's office at the town hall.

'She was only the Town Clerk's daughter,' I thought grimly, 'but she let the Borough Surveyor.'

I only hoped for his sake the bearded clerk didn't turn up at my surgery with a boil to be lanced.

Pam finished the play's run triumphant. She'd been a great success in the part, and there were demands for her to appear in the next production. But the whole five weeks had left me an exhausted wreck. I didn't know whether I could stand any more of it.

'Pam,' I said – as we got to bed after a party with the cast, at which everybody had gone round kissing everybody and calling everybody *Darling* – 'it's all a bit too much for a simple GP. I vastly admired you in your first two productions – Paul and

Trevor – but I can't be certain that I am quite as delighted with this latest production.'

'Oh, goody,' said Pam. 'You mean we should concentrate on more children?'

9

Death of a Child

For the first two or three years after the birth of Paul, life was at its best. I couldn't remember there ever being a better time. I cannot recall anything bringing more joy than having children of my own, and watching them grow up.

Pam's father, Gerry, retired. He and Pam's mother, May – who for some reason we always called Bill – came to live at Winchcombe. They were always prepared to come and babysit or look after the children when we went away on holiday.

Bill was a marvellous person. She was crippled with arthritis, always in pain, and had had two major operations on her hips. This was before the days of artificial hip replacements. In spite of her pain, she was never down in spirits and was a wonderful help to Pam with the growing boys.

Gerry settled down in this new area, fishing, shooting, and occasionally dragging me out for a game of golf.

Herbert Barlow would also babysit for us at any time. He acted as an uncle to the two boys. After a series of marriages, Herbert had lost touch with his own children and my boys took the place of the family he used to have.

He was a great asset to the household. He made toys for the children and was instrumental in getting Paul to start walking by making him a wheeled contraption with which he could propel himself round. As well as making household furniture, Herbert was a skilled tailor – a legacy of the days when he stage managed in the theatre – and would make dresses for Pam and shirts for me from offcuts of material he picked up in the market.

With the children and home secure, we were able to take a marvellous holiday with Janice and Kevin Bird.

My Morris Minor, the first car that I had owned, I had run into the ground. It was like losing an old friend but I was very proud of my new A40, with its Italian-designed body, the first of its kind in Tadchester.

We loaded the A40 to bursting point and drove to Newhaven. There we watched my precious car being swung by crane on to the boat, to pick it up at Dieppe and then drive down through France and Spain to a villa we had hired in Loret del Mar.

Knowing that we would be staying in the villa for most of the holiday, we had taken the bare essentials, and had a hilarious time camping on the way down.

I had left Kevin to equip us with a tent, and at our first camping site I saw it for the first time. It was a small, square, ridge pole tent, spotlessly white, somehow typically British, and to emphasise this had a Union Jack sewn firmly on its side.

The sleeping arrangements were quite hysterical. The four of us could just squeeze into the tent, lying side by side. There was no slack space to be taken up. If one turned during the night, it meant we all had to turn. Janice and Kevin were going through one of their heavier periods at that time and could muster about twenty-eight stone between them.

The French and other Continentals on the camping sites, with all their sophisticated camping gear, used to look in amazement as four people rolled out of this tiny tent. Through the day they watched every move that we made in total disbelief. A Frenchman with a tent opposite ours used to eat his meals outside with his eyes glued on us. He would shovel food into the corner of his mouth furthest away from us so that his feeding hand never interfered with his vision. Once he became so engrossed that a forkful of food finished up in his ear.

Kevin and I, early one evening, decided to go fishing. We asked the girls for the stale bread we knew we had, for bait, to be

84

told that it had already been thrown away. Followed by the startled eyes of our conscientious watcher opposite, Kevin and I walked to the waste bin, fished out a loaf of bread, and walked back to the tent. Our onlooker's eyes nearly dropped from their sockets. *Les pauvres Anglaises*! Obviously things in Britain were worse than he'd suspected.

When we returned from our fishing trip we found Janice flaked out on an airbed outside the tent with Mediterranean tummy. Our faithful Briton-watcher was nodding his head knowingly. That's what happens when you start eating bread you have picked out of the dustbin . . .

Our villa in Loret del Mar was luxurious and terribly cheap, as were food, wine and cigars, particularly cigars. I could buy six large ones for a shilling.

Loret at this time was a small Spanish fishing town, with new hotels only just beginning to appear. We had a marvellous holiday, swam in the Mediterranean, cooked barbecues in the garden of our villa, and stocked ourselves up with local leather produce — shoes, slippers and handbags — and filled all the empty spaces in the boot with bottles of wine for the journey home.

We went back via Paris, camped the last two nights in the Bois de Boulogne, and had a day's sightseeing around that magical city.

We split up in Paris, each couple going their own way. Pam and I went to some art galleries and up the Eiffel Tower with just enough money left for what we thought would buy us a small meal. Pam was dying for a cup of tea. It turned out to be the price of the small meal we had so looked forward to. All we had to eat for the day was an omelette that we shared between us.

It was obvious that we weren't as clever with our money as Janice and Kevin. When we came back to the tent in the evening to rejoin them, we had to listen to their description of the three marvellous meals they had eaten that day, which included oysters, steaks, wines and gateaux. It was too much for me. I sprang on an old crust of French bread lying in the corner of the tent and devoured it. This time I really was *le pauvre Anglais*.

We returned from our holiday bronzed and happy, and picked up the boys from their grandparents. They had had such a good time they were almost loath to come away. We came back to our flat to find that Herbert had not only a meal ready for us, but had filled the house with flowers. Life was really beautiful.

Back in Tadchester we saw a great deal of Eric and Zara. Eric and I both fancied ourselves as cooks. We used to take it in turn to produce exotic meals, with Pam and Zara sitting back happily enjoying our various culinary efforts.

We went fishing on the beaches with Frank and Primrose, and introduced Phil and Joan to this new art. I was very heavily involved with the Round Table and all their festivities, carnivals, parties; there didn't seem a minute to spare. Life was full and I couldn't wish to live in a better place, surrounded by better people. I got on well with my partners and enjoyed both the practice and the hospital work. It was a glorious summer that year and we spent as much time as we could on the beach and in the sea. It looked as if the good things would go on for ever. But I was to learn . . .

*   *   *

Amongst my medical duties I shared the emergency anaesthetics with Jack Hart, week in and week about. Henry Johnson made himself available to do the emergency surgery practically all the time; just occasionally he allowed one of the Winchcombe surgeons to deputise and give him a night off.

I was called one weekend by Henry to the hospital to give an anaesthetic in an emergency operation. 'A bad one here, Bob,' said the gruff Henry. 'You may need Jack Hart to give you a hand.'

Jack and I shared the emergency anaesthetics but whenever there was a difficult case we worked in tandem. Two pairs of hands were better than one if somebody was very ill and drips and intravenous transfusions had to be put up.

I went to the hospital straight away, and was shown a delightful three-year-old, golden-haired boy. He was obviously very ill, with acute appendicitis and peritonitis. He was in a very poor condition and it was going to be a fight to get this little lad through.

It was part of the duties of all of us to give anaesthetics when required, but none of us was fully trained as a qualified anaesthetist. Each year I used to go back to my teaching hospital to do a couple of weeks of anaesthetics to keep me up with the latest trends, but there was always the possibility that there might be some technique that I didn't know.

This used to worry me, but Jack Hart was always a great comfort. He'd been giving anaesthetics for many years and had never had any trouble.

The anaesthetics available for children in those days were very limited, and consisted mainly of a mixture of chloroform and ether. We didn't have all the wonderful new relaxant drugs that are available now.

This little mite was all togged up ready for his operation. He looked like a little golden-haired elf. As we came to him (and it was the only time it ever happened to me in medicine) he put his arms up and said, 'Can I kiss you, Doctor Daddy?' Jack and I both had to be kissed by this little chap before we could start the anaesthetic.

The boy was very ill all through the operation. Henry, working quickly, removed the offending appendix. He was stitching up when the little boy collapsed and began to behave in a way that I'd never known an anaesthetised patient behave before.

He started to convulse. It was a very muggy night and the theatre was hot, so we began to cool him by spongeing him down. His condition deteriorated and we started all the procedures available for the resuscitation of a collapsed patient. I put a tube into his lungs and began mechanically to respire him. Although I could keep him going, he didn't appear to improve. Henry rang for the consultant anaesthetist from

Winchcombe to come over, and we continued with our respiring.

Slowly the little boy began to respond. His colour improved, but he was not able to maintain his breathing without help. I was very relieved when the consultant anaesthetist from Winchcombe arrived and took over the whole situation.

He changed the tube that I had put into the lungs for a bigger one. As he did so, the little patient collapsed again. We couldn't find his pulse and the colour drained from him. We tried all the methods of resuscitation – cardiac massage, oxygen, injections – to no avail.

The little patient died.

I couldn't believe it. This was the appealing, golden-haired elf who, only an hour earlier, had insisted upon giving me a kiss.

Life from this point on became an absolute nightmare.

I had to go and break the news of the boy's death – he was an only child – to his parents. Though I broke the news to them as gently as I could, it was naturally all too much for them. They ran screaming round the room, howling dementedly like stricken animals. It was some time before I was able to get them to take a sedative, and the only effect that had was to change their howls of grief into deep, painful sobs.

Over the weeks, I had to give the parents as much support as I possibly could. Daily I grieved, not only for the little boy, but for the parents, and for myself. This was the sort of thing that happens only to other people.

The post-mortem examination revealed that the little boy had died of ether convulsions. This is a situation that usually happens only in the tropics and would never happen in this day and age with such different anaesthetics and modern techniques.

I had to go through the harrowing ordeal of a coroner's court, give evidence, and look after the distraught parents when the hearing was over. The verdict was that death was brought about through natural causes and no blame was put on the doctors. On the contrary, we were praised for our efforts. But that was small consolation . . .

*　　　*　　　*

I could not get over the death of the little boy. I began to question myself, to question medicine, and was prepared to tell my tale of woe to anyone. All the time the memory of those screaming parents horrified me.

I somehow got through my work. I used to come home and sit staring into space, or leafing through the *British Medical Journal*, looking for jobs. I hardly spoke to Pam and ignored the children who, sensing something awful had happened, kept quiet and went off to play out of sight whenever I came in. I just didn't know how I was going to get through this one.

Henry Johnson called me into his surgery two weeks after the death.

'Bob, lad,' he said, 'I want you to anaesthetise a case for me this afternoon. And I want you to anaesthetise for me regularly for the next few weeks.'

I realised what he was trying to do, but the thought of it terrified me.

As he said he would, Henry called on me for every anaesthetic case that came in. Each operation was an absolute agony for me. I would sit by the bedside after the patients had been returned from theatre, waiting until they became conscious again. Every anaesthetic I gave was a nightmare, but I had to sit it out and sweat it through.

Always Jack Hart was somewhere in the background, stepping in and keeping an eye on things. And there was always Henry Johnson saying, 'Come on, lad. You're doing fine.' But after every successful operation the old grief returned.

It was Steve Maxwell, my senior partner, who finally got me on my feet again. All the way through he had been a comforting, reassuring presence. He had shared my duties with the bereaved parents, giving the special comfort that he exuded from his own personality.

'Bob,' he said, 'the time has come to be firm with you. You've had your agonies, but we all have them. Henry has to suffer the loss of a patient perhaps once a month – a patient for whom he has done all he can to keep alive. Some things are beyond us and we have to accept them.

'You have nothing to reproach yourself for. You have to get up and about again, and live normally. It's not fair to Pam, the patients, your children, or the practice.'

It was the first time I had heard Steve speak sternly, if that is what it could be called. It really shook me. I mumbled an apology.

'Forget it,' he said. 'Just get out and get on with your work. Try and get back to being the happy man you were before this happened.'

Steve's talk was a tremendous help. With time, I slowly got back into the swing of things. But I never enjoyed anaesthetics again. Eventually, as Winchcombe Hospital grew, more full-time surgeons were appointed and their full-time consultant anaesthetists were in attendance. One of these anaesthetists had to spend half his time at Tadchester and after twelve-months I was able to give up anaesthetising.

But as long as I live I shall never ever forget the small golden-haired boy, who reached out and said, 'Can I kiss you, Doctor Daddy?' just before I was to put him to sleep, into a sleep from which he was never going to wake . . .

10

Soliloquy at Evening Surgery

The death of that child had shattered me almost irrevocably.

For months I went over and over again in my mind the sequence of events of that dreadful day, tracking back over every detail of the operation in an attempt to discover if and where I had made a mistake. I think that subconsciously I *wanted* it to be my fault. Taking the burden of guilt might be some kind of atonement, even some sort of reparation to the parents for the agony of their grief.

I was within an ace of giving up medicine altogether, of going back down the coal-mines where I had served my time as a Bevin Boy, of going into retreat, of becoming a missionary: of doing any one of a dozen things which would take me away from this awful and awesome area of responsibility and allow me to pay at least some of the debt I felt I owed.

But, being as critical as I could of myself, my colleagues, the equipment and the procedures of the operation, I could not lay blame. It was literally a million-to-one chance. There was the combination of warm, muggy weather, a little-known side effect of ether, and a constitutionally susceptible patient. With hindsight, it appeared that the child might well have reacted the same way, whatever the weather. But then there was no way of telling. And now there was no way of knowing.

It is a rare general practitioner who is unaffected by death, familiar as it becomes over the years. The loss of a patient – even of one whose illness is obviously terminal, or whose life has run well beyond its allotted span – is a personal loss. Afterwards, there are always the self-doubts, the silent questions. Could I have done more? Could I have spotted the signs any earlier? Dare I have risked one of the new drugs whose possible adverse effects were not yet proven?

In the professional life of every GP there is always at least one death which shakes him to the roots of his being: a death totally unexpected, and often inexplicable, of someone who had every reason and every right to live.

I have not laid the ghost of that child, nor ever will. What I *have* been able to do, with time, is to come to some sort of terms with it. Some sort of terms, too, with the whole of my medical work.

It is easy for a general practitioner to feel depressed. He has a strenuous working life, with a high responsibility factor, spent entirely in contact with sick people. His company is sought only by the unwell. If somebody is happy, healthy, coping, achieving or being successful by any definition at all, he does not seek out his doctor.

In his blacker moments a GP can see himself living in a half world in a half light, populated by ailing, inadequate and often hopeless people. In a seemingly endless stream, these people come along and raid his own physical, mental and emotional reserves, which by the end of the day are almost always near to exhaustion anyway.

Often, at the end of an evening surgery, I will spend a few quiet minutes mentally soliloquising, recapitulating on the day and getting things back into perspective.

A great help in dealing with a pompous, arrogant or aggressive patient whose personality is threatening to overwhelm the whole consultation, is the advice given to me once by an uncle: imagine him sitting on the toilet. Suddenly, this loud, overbearing, perhaps nasty piece of work, is reduced to human scale and I can concentrate on the real issue of what ails him.

If I am treating a nice character, a good character, an honest, hard-working, cheerful or creative one, I can think beyond the actual treatment to the life-style of the patient, and feel glad that I am making some contribution to its comfort or continuance. When I am injecting the piles, say, of an artist – be he writer, painter, sculptor, musician or singer – I think of the joy of his art, not of the sordid job of the moment.

Faced with the piles of a character towards whom I feel antipathetic – one of the pompous, arrogant or aggressive ones perhaps – I am faced simply with piles. These I treat competently, professionally and gently. But one third, perhaps even two thirds, of my mind is metaphorically looking out of the window.

During the mechanical procedure of treatment the saving third of my mind is busy in my garden, mending my seine fishing net, casting a spinner across the nose of a lurking salmon, making a golf shot or composing a speech for a Rotary dinner.

Now and again I get some really bad hat as a patient and I wonder why I am taking all this trouble. A wife-beater, perhaps, with fibrositis of the right shoulder. I treat him, make him well – and for what? To be fit enough to beat his wife again?

According to the Hippocratic Oath, of course, I should not be asking questions like this. But now and again even Hippocrates must have wondered what it was all about.

Many patients do not come for treatment of a physical ailment, even if they have managed to produce a physical or psychosomatic condition as the excuse. They come because they want to be told what to do. They have reached a point of stagnation or unease in their lives and they want advice. The cause of the unease can be almost anything – money, sex, marriage, career, life-style – and often they themselves do not know. But they feel uneasy and they come along in the expectation of a magic formula which will solve the problem.

Even if they are not sure of the question, they want an answer. I don't know the answer. They don't know the answer. Possibly there is no answer. But I am expected to give it.

The common denominator of such patients is that they lack direction. All I can do is to point them in one. It may not be the direction in which they want to go. Often it has to be a short term direction, such as just clearing off for at least forty-eight hours to a place they have never visited before. But any direction is better than none. It breaks the pattern in which they have become trapped. It gives them a view from the outside of their own condition and surroundings. It breaks the inertia in which they have been sitting perhaps for years. It gives them some momentum. They are on the move again. And once on the move, they are much better fitted to find a direction of their own.

*   *   *

So often I sit there after evening surgery, checking on my own bearings, adjusting my own direction.

I have no authority, other than that which my medical skills command. I have no wisdom, other than that which I have acquired slowly and often painfully over the years. I have no sincerity – no, perhaps that's not quite fair.

I feel the lack of sincerity when I have to make tactful pronouncements about a condition which is self-inflicted. I cannot tell patients that they are suffering from whatever because they are idle, greedy, self-indulgent, neglectful or weak willed. I cannot say to an overweight woman, convinced that the trouble lies in her 'glands': 'You are fat because you are greedy. You eat too much. Eat less. And get off your backside and do some work for a change.' I have to be diplomatic, couch the diagnosis in phrases which would do credit to an ambassador, and break the terms of the cure more gently.

Often I have to tell an outright lie about a condition: perhaps a cancer which may or may not respond to treatment, but with the knowledge of which the patient would obviously not be able to cope. This is not really insincerity: it is tailoring the revelation to the mental or emotional resilience of the patient.

For some of the time I *can* be sincere. I can tell a patient straight, and without beating about the bush, what is wrong and what the treatment will involve. Patients such as these – and sometimes one has to be almost a mind reader to judge – do a lot to restore one's faith in humanity.

But for much of the time I look upon myself as an insincere Solomon, reaching into the reserves of my energy, doling out handsful of my own substance in an effort to keep people on the move. I realise that with some individuals the limit of my achievement is to assist them over a stile, knowing that my help will only last until the next stile. If they can't get over that one unaided, they'll be back again for another piece of me.

However much I would like to, I cannot swim around the great lake of life supporting people in the water. All I can do is to throw lifebelts to some who look as if they might drown.

Sometimes the soliloquy takes all sorts of odd turns. I can recognise quality in people, but am not articulate enough to name it. I believe that hard work is the salt of life and that without it everything would lose its savour. Some days I seem to know all there is to know, but most days I know nothing at all.

So it goes on, in those few precious minutes of quietness after evening surgery. The thinking is often not logical, seldom conclusive, but it does help to loosen the grip of tension and blow away the mists of depression.

In recognising tension and depression after a gruelling day's work, I am naming the villains. Once named, they lose their power. I begin to recognise in the people of the day all sorts of qualities I had not noticed before, and they rise in stature as the recognition dawns.

Slowly my equilibrium returns. And by stepping on the jumble of my thoughts, climbing over the mental and emotional debris of an exhausting day, I have risen a plane. I can once again see the beauty and purpose of all things. And leave the excreta of my mind behind.

Can't I go Down the Mine, Daddy?

Thudrock Colliery was to close. The announcement in the *Tadchester Echo* came as a tremendous blow to the town. Most of the Thudrock work force came from Tadchester and formed a sizeable part of the working population.

The original shaft of Thudrock had been sunk in 1905 and the pit had continued to produce coal uninterruptedly for more than fifty years. Now the coal was getting more difficult and more expensive to get out and the National Coal Board decided to close the colliery.

The closure was to be phased over a period of six months. Although people had felt for some time that this was likely to happen, although there had been lots of coming and going by high officials in the Coal Board, nothing had actually been said and now the whole community was stunned.

There were still a few old-timers who could remember the days before the mine was there, but for the vast majority it had always existed as an essential and integral part of the area. The pit buses used to travel the six miles to and from Tadchester Market Place every hour. I had held a surgery at Thudrock ever since I came to Tadchester, and with the mine closing this small, primitive outpost of medicine would be closing too.

It was interesting that all the miners I ever met, both at

Thudrock and during my own mining days, said they hated coal mining and would do anything to get out of it. Now that the pit was closing, however, it appeared that coal mining was the only thing most of them wanted to do.

I had been a Bevin Boy just after the end of the war and had worked on the coal face for two years. Although the conditions were indescribable and the work extremely hard and difficult in the most uncomfortable surroundings, mining had a dignity and sense of adventure about it, and I would consider coal face workers much in the same way that I do mountaineers. They are fighting the elements, pitting themselves against Nature. The coal face was only as safe as the worst workman on it, and there was a unity and comradeship among coal face workers of the kind found only among men in hazardous callings.

There was little alternative employment in Tadchester. In the rather short summer season, various jobs could be found in the holiday industry, but in the winter there was no other real basic industry for men to work at. On the individual, personal level it was bad enough to see a huge collier having to change from hacking away at the coal face to selling ice-cream or tending deck-chairs on the front, but for the town it was a major disaster. There were protest meetings, suggested sit-ins,

letters to the MP, and a campaign conducted by the local paper. Finally one of the complicated Government inducements to industrial firms was offered for the Tadchester area. An electronics factory opened near the coal mine. Just after work started on the site, one of the big international chemical companies decided that there was still some life in the slag heaps that surrounded the village of Thudrock and Thudrock Colliery, and put forward plans to build some huge works to convert the slag heaps into plastic. Apparently Thudrock slag had special qualities that slag heaps at other collieries didn't have.

Over a period of two to three years, both the electronics factory and the plastics factory were in full production. The electronics factory employed more women than men, but the plastics factory employed more people than had ever worked down Thudrock Colliery. But something had gone from the area. The ruggedness of the local miners seemed to disappear when they went to work in clean clothes, some wearing collars and ties. That, coupled with the decline of the fishing industry – only two boats still fished out of Tadchester – changed the character of the area and it became more suburban.

These changes didn't affect the farming community. The farmers were a sturdy, independent lot, and I got to know many of them in the Tadchester Market through my friend Kevin Bird, who was employed by a firm of agricultural auctioneers.

Kevin had been originally farm manager to the de Wyrebocks. Commander and Mrs de Wyrebock had presided over a large house and a huge estate. On the death of Commander de Wyrebock, Mrs de Wyrebock moved away to live with her daughter and son-in-law. Her daughter, Marjorie – whose teeth were almost as large as those of the horses she rode so well – was one of the problems, emotional and medical, that I had to cope with in my earlier days in the practice. I was lucky to escape the altar, the fate that Marjorie had in mind for me.

When the estate was broken up it was bought up by some huge London farming consortium. Kevin didn't relish the prospect of working for someone else on a farm he had managed for years, so he looked around for another job. He was soon snapped up by one of the local agricultural auctioneers and did most of the auctioning in the Tadchester Market.

The cattle market was situated down near the riverside. It had been built since the war, and had well-designed stalls and comfortable accommodation for sheep and cattle. Its one big disadvantage was that it was away from most of the pubs. The old market had been near the pannier market in the upper part of the town. There was a large square which was half pannier market, half cattle market and surrounded by shops and pubs.

I don't think that the publicans minded the moving of trade: in fact the effects were barely noticeable. Tadchester got so crowded on market day that it was hardly worth taking your car into the town. By the time the farmers and traders had walked to the pubs from the new market they were thirstier than they were in the good old days when they could step from the market straight into the pub. Anyway, no-one grumbled.

The farming community had always steered clear of the mining community, and when the colliery closed they each still went their separate ways. Very few of the colliers looked for jobs in farming. Although they had complained for years about the horrors of working underground, they'd got so used to it that the thought of working out in the open didn't appeal to them.

The only times the farmers and miners really got together were at the point-to-point meetings. The local farmers' point-to-point race meetings were held in the spring and late autumn. It was traditional for the colliery to shut down on the first Monday in May and the first Monday in October, and the two days were real festive occasions. The October holiday was also timed to coincide with the Tadchester Agricultural Show.

The Show was held later than most agricultural shows but for some strange reason always was blessed with good weather. If you wanted to make sure that your holiday week had good weather, you timed it to coincide with Tadchester Agricultural Show. But if you went away on holiday you missed the Show and that – along with the annual Tadchester Fair, Rowing Regatta and the Cattle Show – was an annual event no Tadchesterian would miss.

There were equestrian events at the Agricultural Show and some of the best riders in the land took part. One or two locals had reached the top in this particular sport and one from near Dratchet had actually been in the British 1948 Olympic show-jumping team.

I had to take Henry Johnson's place as Medical Officer to the Agricultural Show this year. Henry had been asked by the Town Council to be Mayor of Tadchester for one year: a great compliment. Normally only Council members were elected Mayor under some order of seniority. This particular year the rival factions in the Council both put up a man. Neither would accept the other's choice, so it was decided to go outside the Council and Henry was chosen.

*   *   *

With Henry Johnson as Mayor we were short handed in the practice and decided to engage a locum. We found a retired army medical officer who had spent most of his days practising medicine in East Africa.

Dr Jumbo Edwards was a huge man in his late sixties. Somehow he fitted himself into a huge old Humber car which was crammed with medical samples, bottles of medicine, cases, cardboard boxes and a whole variety of other odds and ends.

He became noted for his two favourite questions. As well as exploring somebody medically, he would ask for the spelling of a set of difficult words. They were so difficult that apparently only about two per cent of the population got them right in their first attempt. Jumbo also had a standard question he liked to ask farmers, which was: 'Are a cow's ears in front or behind its horns?'

If a patient was not too ill and had time on his hands, struggling through the spelling was quite fun. With the question about the cows' horns and ears, he had a fifty per cent chance of getting it right. But I began to have complaints. There were patients who were gasping for air with pneumonia, whose lips had turned blue and who thought their last moment had come – and who, instead of being given oxygen or a penicillin injection, were submitted to a spelling test.

One farmer's wife said, 'There was my husband, nearly at death's door. He'd had a coronary and we were waiting for the ambulance – and Dr Edwards kept on asking which was in front on a cow's head, the ears or the horns. My husband couldn't answer – he was almost unconscious. Why couldn't Dr Edwards go and look at a cow and find out for himself?'

While we were being helped out by Dr Jumbo, part of Tadchester Bridge fell away and was out of action for three months. This cut the town in two and separated the westward part of the town from the world in general. By car you could get to the other side of the river only by doing a twenty-five-mile detour round country lanes through Dratchet, but you still were allowed to walk across the bridge. So the practice hired a car to keep on the Up-the-Hill side of the bridge. We left our cars on the Down-the-Hill side then walked across to use the other car.

One day when Dr Jumbo was on duty, he was called Up-the-Hill to see some cases. The first was a patient who lived in a cottage at the far end of a wood yard that stretched for a mile along the banks of the Tad. It was quite close to the bridge so Jumbo spurned the use of the car on the other side. It would have been difficult to get his six-foot-two, eighteen-stone frame into it anyway. He set off in the rain with his case in his hand. The wood yard seemed to go on and on. It was raining heavily, Jumbo wasn't as young as he used to be, and his case got heavier with every step.

By the time he got to his call, Jumbo was soaked through and exhausted. The patient he had called to see had to rub him down, dry his clothes, give him tea and brandy, get out his own car and drive him to the other two visits on that side of the river.

It was too much for poor Jumbo: he was in bed for a fortnight with a chest infection. Reluctantly he resigned from his locum and went back to do a three-month spell in the sunnier climes of his beloved East Africa. We could all imagine him out there, still asking silly questions about cows' ears – and setting tricky spelling problems in Swahili.

*   *   *

We were fortunate enough to get as a replacement a young, newly qualified Oxford running blue, called Ron Dickinson. He stayed on after Henry's term of office, becoming junior partner and increasing our number to five.

The plastics factory had brought more labour into the town and the practice had expanded to the extent that we needed an extra pair of hands. Steve Maxwell had indicated that he didn't want to do quite as much as he used to do, and had begun to cut down.

Ron Dickinson was one of the most athletic men I have ever met. He was always bouncing about, involved in every athletic pursuit that the local area had to offer. He would run with the harriers, play rugby, cricket, sail, swim, water-ski and play squash. If he was ever missing, a quick ring round the local sporting establishments would soon find him.

It was disconcerting in later years, when we'd built a house just outside Tadchester by the river, to look out of the window and see Ron go by on his water skis. Pam would look at me quizzically.

'Who's on duty?'

'Oh, Ron,' I'd say. 'I think I must have said I'll stand in for him.'

*   *   *

Henry made a magnificent job of Mayor. He was always a good speaker: in fact the difficulty usually was in stopping him speaking. The one problem was that, at over six foot, he was taller than most mayors. Although some of the regalia had to be made for him, Tadchester couldn't fully re-equip him for just one year, so some of the mayoral garb was a bit short in the sleeves. The beaverskin hat worn traditionally by the Mayor – a remnant of Tadchester's ancient link with the Newfoundland cod trade – was far too small for him.

Henry flagged a bit towards the end of his year. He was still doing some work at the surgery and some operating at the hospital. Seeing him looking pale at the end of surgery one day, I enquired what the matter was.

'Sauterne and bloody chicken, lad,' he replied.

Henry had worked out that of the 220 dinners he had been to during the year he had Sauterne wine and chicken at 120.

Young Ron fitted well into the practice and had the same problems as I had with lady suitors when I first arrived in Tadchester. Most of his admirers seemed to come down from London, whereas mine had been local. After a couple of years of struggling to maintain his independence he succumbed and married Jeanette Upton, a delightful daughter of one of the local bank managers.

Although Steve Maxwell had said he was reducing his work, he still came in every Sunday. He decided that as he was reducing his work he ought to reduce his holidays. So he took a fortnight's less holiday than we did and he now lived outside Tadchester with old Dr Watts and his wife. Dr Watts had been the senior partner before Steve.

Dr and Mrs Watts had a few acres of ground that Steve used to work on with all sorts of modern agricultural devices. He never seemed to want to go too far away on holiday. He used to say that he would plant his potatoes in his first fortnight's spring holiday, and spend the second fortnight of his leave in the autumn digging them up. He always remained the same selfless smiling Steve, and looking after his potatoes was all the leisure activity he ever seemed to want to do.

We were all invited with our wives to Henry's final mayoral banquet. Ron, still single at this time, and by far the junior member of the practice, was full of beer at the end of the lengthy speeches. It seemed that anybody and everybody remotely connected with the mayoral office in the town had spoken. Then Ron got up, staggered towards Henry, clutching a brown box, and said, 'A special remembrance present Mr Mayor, from your junior partner.'

Henry opened the box with some embarrassment – and found two unplucked chickens, tied carefully round a bottle of Sauterne . . .

12

Creatures of Habit

I would not have missed for anything my weekly philosophical chats with Bob Barker at the bookshop at Sanford-on-Sea. He had great wisdom and most times I visited him he would take up a subject and then would explore it.

One day, as usual, his smiling face looked over the desk at me.

'Coffee and a cigar, Bob?' he said – he had obviously been waiting for me to come – and launched forth with today's subject: 'Creatures of Habit'.

'I've always marvelled at the part habit plays in people's lives,' said Bob. 'So many people have a daily, weekly, monthly, annual rhythm which it would be unthinkable to break. More than a few even set the rhythm in advance, planning out their lives over the foreseeable future, listing how every penny is to be spent, where they are going for their holidays, when they are going to change the car, what they will do when the children leave home, and where they will retire to. Their life is patterned out completely before them.

'To some extent it's like the man who learns to drive a bus round a particular route. He knows that from then on he can do this route for the rest of his life, and the only thing he has to do is to keep his nose clean.

'This,' said Bob, 'horrifies me. Take away life's unpredictability, take away all the surprises, know exactly what tomorrow will bring, and what have you left, except a long long yawn? But

I must admit that a lot of people like it that way and seem to prosper on it even if they never are the life and soul of the party.

'When disaster strikes such people they react in different ways. Some refuse to believe that their ordered pattern could possibly be interfered with. You have a situation, say, where the husband comes in and says, "Darling, bad news. The cat's dead." The wife replies, "Impossible, she's only five years old." "Yes," says the husband, "but the lorry didn't know that."

'Other people finding themselves faced with something which was not in their forward planning just go to pieces. It is as if some central nerve has been cut and all the other parts of their life pattern can do nothing but flop around in an uncoordinated and quite bizarre way. Others just ignore any kind of disaster and go on as if nothing had happened. For some it's a life saver, for others it's a bit like the chap whose bicycle had been stolen from outside the house. He was so used to it being there that he rushed out that morning, leapt gaily into the saddle and fell flat on his face.'

I went along with Bob only so far.

'Come off it, Bob,' I said. 'Most people have to find a formula for survival. They form a habit pattern so that there is something they can depend on: they are just not of the disposition to cope beyond a certain area and they are wise living within the confines of their own limitations. Habit is their stabiliser.

'Housewives, for instance, get into a routine while the children are young, feeding, washing, shopping, cleaning, and cooking. This routine is very necessary for the orderly functioning of the household. When circumstances sometimes change, the routine can be hard to break. I have known wives who, for months after the children left home, went on cooking the same amount of food for meals. It resulted in a lot of waste or a great increase in the weight of the parents. Or even chronic indigestion or constipation for both husband and wife.

'At this stage, with their habit broken, people will often produce some medical infirmity. It is a true and real one and it provides something to hide behind. The whole basis of such an illness could possibly be self-induced and I think more and more doctors should treat the whole patient rather than treat the disease: the disease is probably a reflection of the person's situation and state of mind, economic circumstances or whatever.'

Old Bob chuckled. He said, 'I remember our neighbour Lucy Parker was due to go on holiday with her husband and baby son. She had washed, ironed, packed, got everything ready for departure. When the taxi arrived outside the house the breakfast pots had not been washed.

' "Come on," said her husband, who in fairness to Lucy had not done a lot to help. "If we don't leave this second we'll miss the train to Winchcombe and there isn't another to London for hours."

' "I can't leave this house," said Lucy, "until these pots are washed," completely forgetting that the object of the exercise was to get away for a well-earned rest.

' "Look," said her husband, "you get in the taxi with the lad and get the driver to put the cases in. I'll wash the pots and lock up and come out to you."

'Lucy did this, fretting in case her husband didn't wash up properly, but they got away in time to catch their train. That evening in London they decided to have a leisurely stroll up the Mall from Admiralty Arch to Buckingham Palace, then wander in St James's Park and feed the ducks.

'Lucy, with the boy in the pushchair, set off up the Mall at a brisk trot. The husband, who'd been admiring the legs of some Scandinavian girl tourists, suddenly realised this and chased after her.

' "Where are you rushing off to?" he panted. "I don't know," said Lucy – and nor did she. She was so used to rushing round the shops at home, full pelt, that a leisurely stroll now called for a great deal of conscious adjustment.

'However, the holiday did have its effect on Lucy and when she returned home she was a great deal more relaxed. But the tension returned as soon as she opened the kitchen cupboard to make a cup of tea. There before her eyes was a stack of unwashed pots, covered after a fortnight with a green mould and grey fur!

'Her husband had taken the rational man's way out. The holiday was the first priority, the pots didn't matter – so he'd shoved the whole lot dirty into the cupboard and shut the door.'

I followed Bob's story with one about the young husband of a patient of mine. I called him Jack so as not to break any confidences, though Bob didn't know him anyway.

Jack had been brought up in the old tradition of being waited on hand and foot by the womenfolk of the family. As a youngster and as a single man he had never done a stroke of work at home, nor had his father or his brother. When they arrived back from work they ate their meal and stretched out in comfortable chairs in front of the fire.

Mother and sister washed up, brought the coal in – stepping over three pairs of legs to reach the fire – did the ironing and mending, made the supper, and did all the other dozens of things which have to be done.

Jack got married and, although his wife was working full time, assumed that things would remain the same. His wife would lay out his clean clothes in the morning, cook breakfast, wash up, dash off to work in a panic. All Jack ever did was read the morning paper and ask for a cup of tea.

Jack's wife then became pregnant but carried on working. She worked half an hour longer than Jack every day and consequently arrived home after him. One Friday evening in winter, when she was almost seven months pregnant, it snowed heavily. That day she did the week's shopping, scurrying around in her lunch hour and picking up the rest of the food after work. She walked a long way up the hill in a blizzard, aching with cold, and weighed down with two enormous shopping bags.

Meanwhile, back at home, Jack was huddled over a one-bar electric fire with a cup of tea. The fire in the hearth needed lighting, but this was not his job. When he answered the door Joyce stood there, unable to move another step. Seven months pregnant, she was chilled to the bone, aching with fatigue and covered in snow. All she could do was burst into tears.

'Don't just stand there sniffling,' said Jack. 'Where the hell have you been until this time? I've been sitting in here an hour freezing to death, and dying of hunger.'

When Joyce came to see me next morning, I asked her to send Jack along to the afternoon surgery. Jack was in before the end of the *morning* surgery – Tadchester United were playing at home that afternoon, and he wasn't missing the match for anybody.

I kept the lecture short and simple, and direct. Jack was amazed. It had never occurred to him that he could be treating his wife badly at all. From then on, apart from the occasional lapse, he was much more considerate and I like to think that I nipped at least one Andy Capp in the bud.

*   *   *

When I'd left Bob and got on my rounds I thought of many of the other strange creatures of habit who were patients. There was Arnold Bishop, a bachelor, whose Saturdays always followed the same pattern. He would rise early, clean his tiny flat, eat his breakfast, then start his perambulations.

The round was always the same. First: Tadchester covered market. There he would savour the sights and smells of the fruit, vegetables, fish and meat and perhaps buy something for his tea.

Next: Tadchester Museum. After browsing among the exhibits he would go to the toilet: (a) because it was time, (b) because he had a special fondness for the marble and brass fittings of the Tadchester Museum Gents.

Then a promenade up the High Street, mainly window shopping at the antique shops and browsing in the secondhand book shops. At each shop he would spend exactly the same amount of time as he had done every Saturday for years. When shopkeepers saw him approaching in his slow, abstracted way, they would check their watches and adjust them if they did not correspond to Arnold's regular time of arrival.

A wander through the graveyard of Tadchester Parish

Church and a reading of some of the more interesting tomb-stones was followed by a visit to the church itself. A few minutes were spent in silent prayer, followed by an inspection of the brasses.

Then would come Arnold's pub crawl: four pubs in measured succession and a chat with a different set of cronies – but always the *same* different set of cronies – in each.

In each pub, too, he had a different kind of drink. Lager in one, beer in another, red wine in the next and gin and tonic in the last. What this did to Arnold's constitution I shudder to think, but his constitution was also almost certainly a creature of habit, and well able to cope.

What puzzled me was that between the third and last pub, Arnold always took a peculiar route. He would pass the last pub, walk right to the end of the High Street and stand there for five minutes outside the petrol filling station before walking back to make his last call and savour his gin and tonic.

One day when he came to the surgery with his annual stomach upset and very bad sunburn, I asked Arnold about his dog-leg progress to the last pub.

'Ah yes. Of course, *my* dear chap,' he said. 'Before your time on that site used to stand a delightful hostelry called the

Plough, and it was my custom to call there before doubling back to the Dog and Partridge. A few years ago by some fiendish act of chicanery, it was bought up, its licence revoked, demolished, and that monstrous filling station built on the site. I suppose you could call it a sentimental journey . . .'

For a couple of weeks one winter, Tadchester Market was closed for alterations. It completely wrecked two of Arnold's Saturdays. The following Monday morning saw him in my surgery, edgy and twitching, and asking for something for his 'nerves'. Arnold's survival depended on routine.

Even more bizarre than his routine at home were the reasons for Arnold's annual stomach upset and sunburn. During the war, the only interruption in Arnold's life, he'd spent two years with the RAF in Libya. Every year since he'd taken a fortnight's holiday in the same town in which he was stationed, staying in the same hotel in which he was billeted, laying about on the same beaches that he laid about on as an airman.

Arnold did not like Libya, he did not like the people, he did not like the hotel, and couldn't stand the food or wine, nor was he fond of swimming in the sea or lying about on the beach. His skin was sensitive and any exposure to sun brought it peeling off his shoulders. But at least he knew what he did not like.

He knew that he would complain about the same things that he complained about every year, argue with the same hotel

manager. He knew also that his stomach would be dreadfully upset and that his sun-burned skin would cause him agony. If any man ever knew where he stood it was Arnold Bishop, Creature of Habit . . .

*　　　*　　　*

Among other extreme examples of creatures of habit were some of the local freshwater anglers, who were nothing if not set in their ways. A tributary of the Tad, the Dipper, was notorious for its unpredictability as an angling river. Some years there would be no fish caught in it at all, and on 'good' years a few sickly and stunted specimens would be pulled out, to be marvelled at by the regulars on the bank.

The anglers on the Dipper were real regulars who had fished it for years with appalling results, yet who refused to move down to the rich pickings in the Tad itself. 'The Dipper Dafties', John Denton, the water bailiff, used to call them.

During his first year as bailiff, John tried telling them that the water was not worth fishing, but the answer was always the same. They'd fished that river, man and boy, and enjoyed every minute of it; there were bigger fish in there than ever came out, and they were blowed if they were going to join the once-a-year fair-weather fishermen on the Tad.

Please yourselves, thought John, and after that he changed his patter. As he checked the fishing tickets of the old boys and listened to their miserable record of non-catches, he would give a knowing wink and say, 'Ah yes. The fish on this river don't give themselves up.' This pleased the old boys no end. The bailiff knew what they knew. To catch anything in the Dipper you had to be something special, and one day patience and skill would be rewarded.

The problem with the Dipper turned out to be pollution, seepage from some old mineworkings near the headwaters. By the time the water mixed with that of the Tad the pollution was dilute enough to have no effect. But on the narrow Dipper it was a killer.

Eventually, the source of the pollution was traced and dealt with, and the fish started moving up the Dipper again. The regular anglers pulled in some real beauties for a whole season and boasted in the local pubs with many an 'I told you so'.

By next season the word had got round, and the banks of the little river were crowded with strangers. In spite of their big catches the old boys grumbled that there was barely space to cast a line and that their once beautiful banks were being covered with all sorts of litter, that things weren't what they used to be, and never would be again.

From late autumn to early spring, there was almost continuous rain, interrupted only by massive snow falls just after Christmas. The Dipper was scoured by a succession of flash floods and all the fish and most of the vegetation were swept down into the Tad.

When the waters finally subsided the pollution had returned. Floods had broken the seals on the mineworkings and the Dipper was back to normal – not a fish to be had. Through the whole of its length the regulars had it all to themselves again, and they sat there day after day with seraphic smiles on their faces, literally happy not to be catching a thing.

They were like so many of us, particularly as we grow older. We like things predictable, don't want things to change. There's probably a little bit of Arnold Bishop in all of us . . .

13

Sex and Side Effects

Apart from its being a prerequisite of the continuance of the human race, sex has always seemed to me a delightful way of communication and I am grateful for the fact that it's here to stay. But it is surprising how many complex problems it brings to the door of a country practitioner.

Whether the problems are more common in a country practice than in town, I don't know, but I feel that in town people probably have more enlightened attitudes towards – and more access to – the sophisticated side of physical communication between people.

Sex, as mankind's most powerful instinct, is bound to bring problems, but the problems are often not with the instinct or the act itself. Rather do they tend to arise from the deviation of the drive or ignorance of the function. A frightening aspect is the number of people who spend years thinking they are abnormal – perhaps out of ignorance, fear or the result of a repressive upbringing – when all they have is a healthy sex drive which they do not understand or for which they have no outlet.

Joshua Verity was a well built young man, dark-haired and good looking, but he had problems.

'Animal appetites, Doctor,' he whispered, glancing round the consulting room in case anyone was listening behind a filing cabinet. 'That's what I've got.'

'What form do they take?' I asked. 'Over-eating?'

'No, animal appetites. You know – *lust*. Lusts of the flesh. *Women*.'

He said the last word with a shiver.

'How old are you?'

'Twenty-one.'

'And when did you first start noticing these appetites?'

'About five years ago, two years before I went into the army for my National Service.'

'And what form did they take?'

'Thoughts. Wicked thoughts. All about women. And dreams, even worse. Dreadful things started to happen in the night. Awful.'

'Nocturnal emissions?'

'Pardon.'

'Wet dreams?'

'Yes, yes. But I couldn't stop them. I couldn't tell anybody. My parents are members of the Apocalyptic Brethren.'

So that was it. Brought up in a very strict religious sect which had strange views on the most normal of happenings. Poor kid.

'Tell me,' I said, 'what happened when you went into the army? Didn't that change your views?'

'Evil! Oh, it was evil. You've no idea. The language. The behaviour. And the films they showed us about what would happen. Horrible!'

I felt a twinge of sympathy. Films on the danger of VD shown by the army to young men were enough to put anybody off sex for life.

'Did you have sex while you were in the army?'

'Of course not. I would have had to answer to my parents and the church elders when I came back.'

'When you came back, what happened?'

'I couldn't settle at home, especially with the guilt I felt about my appetites. So I left. That was about six months ago. Now I'm in digs in Tadchester and I've got a job.

'I tried group therapy, that didn't work. They tried to get me to confess all sorts of things. They talked to me about libidos and ids and things I couldn't understand.'

'Do you have any friends?'

'Not in Tadchester. No.'

'Girl friends anywhere?'

'No. I can't even talk to girls. My animal appetites overcome me, and I can't speak.'

'Can you dance?'

'No. Dancing is forbidden among the Apocalyptics.'

I had to take a chance.

'Right, Joshua,' I said. 'There is nothing wrong with you except a strong sense of guilt, and a lack of normal social relationships. Your animal appetites are nothing more than a normal young man's sexuality. You are, in other words, just plain randy.'

He looked shocked at first at the bluntness, then an expression of pure relief flooded his face.

'Really?'

'Really,' I said. 'Now what I want you to do is to put yourself into circulation. There are several social clubs in Tadchester. You can get a full list of them from the library. Join one, join several, get yourself moving about among people. Force yourself to talk to them. Above all, listen. You've been drawn in on yourself for too long, now you owe it to yourself to relax a little. Have some fun and make friends.

'Tell you what, on your way out have a chat with Jill, the receptionist. She's a member of one or two clubs and she can advise on what might suit you best. Jill's a girl, I know, but you are asking her on my behalf, not yours. Doctor's orders. No need to feel shy – now off you go.'

It was perhaps wicked of me, but if anybody was to help the boy on his road to normality, it was Jill, my healthily sexed young receptionist at evening surgery. And it worked.

I saw no more of Joshua. But a few months later Jill said, 'Jossy sends his regards, Doctor.'

'Jossy, who's Jossy?'

'You know. The holy man. Or former holy man. You know what they say about convent girls once they're let out? That's nothing to what's happened to old Jossy. If I want to see him

now, I've almost got to book an appointment.'

Well, it may not have been medicine, but my God, did it work . . .

*   *   *

Ignorance, though in a slightly different form, was the problem of a sweet and innocent young engaged couple who came to see me. They were worried because they knew very little about the mechanics of sex and reproduction, and were to be married in a month.

This was way back in the days when sex education at school was skimpy and any child who missed one particular biology lesson could be left in ignorance of everything except what he or she picked up among the sniggers in the school yard. It seems like another age now, but it wasn't really so long ago.

I got them to call back after evening surgery, gave them the basic sex education talk and recommended a manual for newly-weds.

Twelve months later the young wife, Sheila, visited me again.

She was pregnant.

'I see the instruction manual worked all right then,' I joked.

'Oh yes, Doctor, but we did have trouble the very first night. Jim kept having to turn back to page 34 to see if he was doing it properly.'

She realised what she was saying, broke off and blushed deeply.

'Don't worry. More couples than you have had the same trouble,' I said.

'Just one thing worries me, Doctor.'

'What's that then?'

'Are we *really* supposed to do it every night?'

It turned out that husband Jim, once having discovered the knack, had grown really keen on sex and dedicated himself to his art unstintingly. I muttered something about moderation in all things, mutual respect for each other's feelings, and one or two other stock answers. It is difficult to mediate in another couple's love life, especially when oneself is young and newly married.

Sheila passed out of my care for a while into the round of antenatal clinics, relaxation classes and finally to the maternity ward of Winchcombe Hospital where she produced a fine baby.

Jim came to see me two days after the baby was born.

'Excuse me, Doctor' he said, blushing. 'How long is it before I can, we can, start . . . er . . . trying for another family?'

I looked at him, this shy, innocent youth of twelve months ago.

'At least six weeks,' I said.

His face fell.

I thought how different, yet how alike, the two young men were. Jim, the sweet innocent who had had to take his instructions from a book, had turned into a seven-nights-a-week sex machine. And Joshua was the one who had complained about his animal appetites . . .

*   *   *

A really pathetic case was old Norman Singer, the local dirty old man, who'd been convicted a couple of times for offences against young girls. Nothing really vile: the poor old lad wasn't capable of it. But it was certainly upsetting for the girls, and dangerous for Norman if ever his paths were to cross those of the fathers.

He was brought in by Geoff Stansfield, the local probation officer, after being charged with yet another offence.

'I'd like you to look at old Norman,' he said. 'Everybody's yelling "Dirty old man! Hang him!" That kind of thing. But I've spent a lot of time talking to him. He seems quite rational and I am wondering if the problem is something physical, something outside his control.'

I gave old Norman a thorough examination. One or two tests produced odd results, so I referred him to the consultant neurologist at Winchcombe Hospital.

There it was discovered that Norman had some kind of obstruction which was pressing on a nerve which gave him sexual urges of almost uncontrollable magnitude. He was admitted to hospital as a matter of urgency, where a simple operation removed the obstruction.

The operation was quoted by the defence at his trial and Norman was given a conditional discharge. The condition was fulfilled to the end of his life. Norman never molested another child.

I often wonder, when I see cases reported in the more lurid Sunday newspapers, whether if more probation officers followed a case through as thoroughly as Geoff Stansfield, more pathetic old men like Norman might be saved from living their last years in shame or behind bars.

14

Loving Couples

I spent more time than enough in surgery trying to sort out other people's marital problems. So many people came in with so many horrific stories – infidelity, ill-treatment, you name it – that I really began to fear for the future of the whole institution of marriage. Then I came across Mick and Alice, and my faith was restored.

Married fifty years, devoted and loving, Mick and Alice never had much money and never let it bother them. The ideal couple. I asked Mick for the secret of their success. 'A bloody good row at least twice a week,' he said. 'Clears the air something lovely.'

Marital relations became a little strained when Mick retired from his job driving a van for the Tadchester Carpet Service. Alice had a full-time job working for the Tadchester Hospital Canteen and still continued to go out to work.

Mick used to wave her off from the window, a hot mug of tea in his hand, as she trudged off to work through snow, slush, rain or hail.

One night Alice had had enough and combed through the Situations Vacant columns in the *Tadchester Echo*.

'Here you are, Mick,' she said. 'I've found you a job.'

'Give over, woman. I'm retired,' he said.

'You *were* retired,' said Alice. 'Get yourself down there first thing tomorrow and don't wear that flat cap. It's a disgrace.'

'What job is it?' asked Mick.

'Funeral parlour. Driver and pall bearer.'

'Bloody hell.'

'Never mind bloody hell. I'm fed up of going out in all weathers with you standing there with a mug of tea and a silly grin on your face. Besides which it's not good for you to be loafing about all day.'

And so started one of what Mick called the week's bloody good rows.

Next morning, however, Mick set out immaculately dressed in his best suit, overcoat and boots and wearing a velour trilby instead of his favourite flat cap. He even put his teeth in. He was a credit to his loving wife who brushed him down and straightened his tie. Naturally he got the job.

Mick was a bit on the short side and it was a shock at first to see the hearse with Mick's nose underneath a peaked cap just clearing the dashboard. The hearse looked as if it was being driven by an invisible man.

After three weeks Mick came to see me. 'Pulled a muscle in my back I think, Doc,' he said. 'Those flaming coffins weigh a ton. And if there's somebody inside like Sammy Thomas' (the local heavyweight whose corpulence was the cause of his death) 'I've got to shove like mad to stop the thing tilting over and falling on me.'

The problem was that Mick's lack of height made it impossible for him to rest the coffin on his shoulders. To reach the shoulder height of the other pall bearers he had to push upwards with the flat of his hand taking all the strain on his arm and back. I laid him off work for a few days and asked him to mention the problem to the funeral director and the other pall bearers to see if there were any solution.

Next week Mick was back. 'I've done the other side in, Doc,' he said.

'But . . .'

'I know. This you'll never believe.'

'Go on – surprise me.'

'Right,' said Mick. 'I did as you said. Asked if there was a way around the problem of me being so little. They were all very nice and they said yes, change over sides and take the leg end of the coffin. Leg ends are always lighter you see. It worked a treat for a couple of days, carrying on my good side with not much weight.'

'Then what happened?'

'A legless ex-serviceman. Heavy chap. By the time we got to church he'd slid to my end of the coffin. Had to shove like hell to keep him on an even keel and now I'm dicky on both sides.'

That night I called in at Mick's house on my rounds and had a quiet word with Alice. She went through the Situations Vacant columns again and next week Mick was working as a lollipop man outside the local school. With that responsible but not too strenuous job, honour was satisfied all round. Mick had the time to take on a small allotment, providing Alice with fresh vegetables and flowers and giving her considerable pride in her little husband whenever he carried off prizes in the Allotment Society Shows.

* * *

The Golden Wedding celebrations of Mick and Alice ran true to form. They were both staunch Roman Catholics and had given freely of their time and labour. St Malachy's, the Roman Catholic Church, was the youngest of all the religious institutions in Tadchester. It had to fight with innumerable Free Church organisations that had sprung up in the times of John Wesley: Congregationalists, Baptists, as well as the firmly entrenched Church of England and a great number of other, what for a better term could be called, minor religions, such as Christian Scientists, Jehovah's Witnesses, Salvation Army, Seventh Day Adventists, Bible Readers, Gospel Turners, and other sects with obscure names that came and went. Father Daly was the first Parish Priest for St Malachy's and had been in the Church for forty-eight years. Mick and Alice had been married in Winchcombe, but had attended St Malachy's ever since its consecration.

Father Daly decided to give them a surprise for their Golden Wedding and ask them to attend church for a special mass. The special mass was for *them*, and the lovely old couple finished it in tears.

After mass, Father Daly asked the congregation to come round to the church hall for a cup of tea. When they got inside it was more than tea. Tables were laid for a meal. The hall was festooned with bunting and a large placard read 'Happy Golden Wedding, Mick and Alice'. That did it. The tears started again and Mick and Alice saw their food only in a blur.

After the meal, Father Daly gave a speech of congratulations and good wishes. He told of all the help that Mick and Alice had given to the church and the Roman Catholic community in Tadchester. He spoke of what an example their marriage was, what an example they were to everyone present, and what a credit they were to the community. Then he sat down. Alice and Mick sat there with the whole assembly shouting, 'Speech! Speech! Speech!'

Mick by this time was feeling distinctly uncomfortable. To protect himself against the cold in the church he had turned up in his usual winter worshipping outfit: woolly vest and long-johns, woolly shirt, pullover, waistcoat, jacket, overcoat and trousers. He sat down to the meal wearing the lot.

'Take your cap off! Have some respect!' Alice hissed through her tears.

The central heating in the hall was very efficient and Mick was sweating profusely by the time Alice got up to make her speech of reply. Perhaps the heat made him a little tetchy, because twice he interrupted Alice to contradict her on some memory of the past.

'Do that again,' she hissed, 'and I'll fetch you one.'

Mick did it again and Alice fetched him one – a swift clout across the head with her handbag.

The congregation loved it. They rose to their feet applauding thunderously, shouting, 'More! More!'

When Alice finished her speech, Father Daly gave a nod. Somebody switched on the record player in the corner. The hall was filled with the strains of 'Take a Pair of Sparkling Eyes'.

'Ee, Alice,' said Mick.

'Ee, Mick,' said Alice.

The old couple got up, tears running down their cheeks, to take the floor for an anniversary dance. It was a tune which was played by the band in the park when Mick proposed all those years ago, and Father Daly had got to hear of it.

There were beads of sweat on the brows of relatives in the congregation in case Mick had forgotten. But he hadn't, and the old pair celebrated for once without a 'bloody good row'.

*   *   *

Another long-term relationship, but this time as far from marriage as it was possible to get, was that of Major Hawkins and Charlie Sloper. Major Hawkins was everything that his name implied. Tall, erect, brisk in speech, though slowing down in action, well groomed, silver haired and moustached, dressed in tweeds, brogues and always carrying the walking stick with which he had gone over the top several times in World War One.

Charlie Sloper was the complete opposite. The local poacher and ne'er-do-well, diminuitive, smelly, incredibly dirty. Bets had been made in Tadchester about what colour he would be if he ever washed. But the event never happened to settle it. He dressed in a set of holes held together by smelly tatters and the occasional safety-pin.

As a lieutenant, Major Hawkins had been Charlie's platoon officer in the trenches. Charlie, being Charlie, was never out of trouble in the army, and the Major grew sick of seeing his grimy face among the morning defaulters. During an attack, however, so the story went – though nobody had actually heard either man tell it – the Major was blown into a flooded shell hole and would have drowned if Charlie had not jumped in after him and held his head above water until the stretcher bearers arrived.

During the First World War, people from the same community were often in the same army unit. This was particularly true of the village of Altriston just outside Tadchester where the patriotic Lord Tyster had volunteered the whole of his work-force, gardeners, groomsmen on the first day that World War One broke out, and Altriston lost thirty-three of its sons killed in the first world holocaust, all in the Somerset Regiment and most on one dreadful bloody day on the Somme. Altriston had the highest casualty rate of any other comparable village of its size in England. As Bob Barker said, the tragedy of our losses in the First World War was that we lost the cream of English manhood, that the best and ablest volunteers went out there first and were decimated.

The Major and Charlie, both from different walks of life, would have been amongst the first to go abroad. Although they had the comfort of familiar faces around them when they served, they also had the horror of seeing friends and relatives being killed.

Charlie and the Major were both survivors, each in his own way. They'd fought battles to rank and personality during the war, and they fought a running battle of personalities in the later years of their lives. Both basically lonely men, they spent a lot of time in the Tadchester Arms. Strangers who didn't know them thought they hated each other and feared the worst as arguments raged in the public bar.

The choice of location was interesting. These two saw each other twice a day for mutual and ritual insults and the public bar was always the venue. The Major, though accepted and loved by the roughnecks in there, looked distinctly out of place. He really belonged in the saloon among the tweedy county types. Charlie was not allowed in the saloon on the grounds of offending the customers, frightening the horses and generally contravening the germ warfare clauses of the Geneva Convention. So the Major chose the public bar.

It would start as soon as he walked in.

'Here comes Colonel Bogey!' Charlie would shout, and follow it up with a few bars of that well-known military air.

'Ah, Sloper, you squalid little man,' the Major would reply. 'Is that you? I thought you'd be out in the garden blending with the compost heap.'

'Piss orf,' Charlie would reply, the riposte chosen most frequently from the Sloper repertoire of stinging wit.

For an hour or more they would insult each other. The Major's public school accent and studied delivery contrasted strongly with Charlie's wild and obscene utterances.

'Sloper by name and Sloper by nature,' the Major would say. 'Never around when you were needed, always sloping off somewhere. You shouldn't have been drummed out of the army. You should have been fumigated out.'

'Piss orf,' Charlie would reply and follow up with a sophisticated raspberry.

It was worse when they had any real and immediate bone of contention.

*   *   *

Charlie was a natural scavenger. Folk would look out of their bedroom window first thing in the morning and see a diminutive dark shape going through the shrubbery. They would come down to discover that the hens hadn't produced as many eggs as usual, or that there was a gap in their row of cabbages. Sprout plants were bereft of the buttons that only yesterday were there and ready for pickling and there were half a dozen holes in the ground where yesterday there were carrots.

Charlie had kept his army haversack, by now incredibly old, filthy, greasy, and an affront to the Major. The haversack was always full of loot.

One autumn day in the public bar, Charlie rummaged around in the haversack and handed the Major an apple.

'James Grieve that is,' he said. 'Lovely variety, marvellous eating.'

'Ah, yes,' said the Major. 'Delicious. Curiously enough I've got a James Grieve at the bottom of my garden: only a young tree as yet, but it's got enough apples on it to make the picking worth while. I'll have some this evening. Thank you very much for yours, Sloper. Very civil of you, for a change.'

When the Major went out with a basket to harvest his crop

that evening he found only four apples left on the tree. The public bar resounded to accusations and indignant denials, threats of lawsuits, fisticuffs, and pistols at dawn. The Major couldn't prove anything and eventually subsided like a rumbling volcano. Only to erupt again when Charlie, on his way out, tossed him an apple and said, 'Here – have another . . .'

Money was the next bone of contention. One foggy night in the Tadchester Arms, Major Hawkins said, 'Reminds me of the time I lost a whole pocketful of money.'

'Piss orf,' said Charlie. 'You never 'ad a pocketful of money.'

'I'll thank you to keep a civil tongue in your head, Sloper,' said the Major. 'Indeed I had. Seventeen shillings and fourpence, if I remember. I must admit I was a little the worse for wear at the time, having attended the Regimental Dinner from which you were conspicuously absent by popular request. I stopped at the seat at Victoria Corner by the edge of the common. Just to get my breath back and take fresh bearings, you understand.

'When I stood up I lost all the loose change in my trouser pocket. Infernal hole must have crept up on me. Tried to find the old akkers, but in the dark and fog, and all that tussocky grass and stuff, couldn't find a penny. Overnight it snowed heavily, kept snowing for ten days and by the time the stuff had melted there wasn't a penny to be found.'

'How long ago was that?' asked Charlie.

'Good ten years.'

'Going to say,' said Charlie, 'that seat's not been there for five. Vandalised. By vandals, they say. Shoot the bloody lot of them I would.'

By next evening there had been a great deal of scuffing about in the tussocky grass and gorse around the site of the bench at Victoria Corner. In the public bar of the Tadchester Arms Charlie was busy breathing on a collection of assorted coins, and rubbing them vigorously with his off-black handkerchief. The Major came in and after the usual exchange of insults ordered his usual half-pint of bitter.

'On me,' said Charlie.

'Steady on, old chap!'

'I insist.'

'As you will. Most grateful.'

'How much did you say you lost at Victoria Corner all them years ago?' said Charlie.

'Seventeen and fourpence. Why?'

'Either you was mistaken or you was robbed. I could only find eleven and ninepence.'

'You blackguard!' exclaimed the Major. 'Return that money at once!'

''Ow do you know it's yours?' asked Charlie. 'More than you have emptied their pockets at Victoria Corner. All them courting couples for a start must have lost thousands. Treasure trove this is. Anyway shut your row – you've got a half-pint out of it.'

Truth to tell, the Major was not as well off as he seemed. After World War One he went back to a steady but poorly paid job in an estate agents and stayed there until his retirement. True, he now had a detached house with a reasonable bit of garden all paid for and in good condition. But he had to do his share of scrimping and scavenging to keep it going. Especially to please his wife who had married him as a dashing young hero and now thought that perhaps he hadn't made as much of himself as he ought.

*   *   *

The log was the last big argument. The Major had a fireplace which would take logs and there were logs in plenty in the woods around the common. After every high wind the place would be littered with rotten branches and fallen trees. In would go the Major with a length of rope and a ripsaw, muttering to anybody passing, 'Nothing like the old log fires, eh? Nothing like sawing your own: keeps you fit, what?'

He would drag the log home with the rope and put it in his woodshed to dry out sufficiently for use.

One day he came across a beautiful log, left behind from a tree which had been felled by the local council as dangerous.

The council had carted the tree away, but had left a great limb in the undergrowth. The Major trimmed it as best he could, tied a rope around it and tried to drag it away. It wouldn't budge. Dusk was falling and he could not have sawn up the log before dark. He managed to roll it into a hollow, covered it with bracken and left it.

That night in the Tadchester Arms he told Charlie of his find and of his cleverness in concealing the log, to be sawn up later. Next morning he arrived with his saw, and his log was gone.

Lunchtime at the Tadchester Arms that day was quite an event. The Major went for Charlie with his walking stick, using it as if it were a sword. Charlie used his own knobbly stick as if it were a quarterstaff. The two went at it out of the public bar and around the garden for twenty minutes, by which time both had run out of puff and called a halt.

Never once did Charlie admit taking the log, but John Denton gave the game away a few weeks later. He told me about meeting Charlie at first light struggling to tie one end of the log to his ancient bicycle and how he had given Charlie a hand to carry it home.

'For God's sake, John, do me a favour and don't mention it to anyone else,' I said. 'I almost had two coronaries on my hands over that log. If the truth gets to the Major I am going to have a corpse on my hands. A dirty little smelly one.'

Four or five years later when the log incident had passed into local folklore, the Major collapsed in the public bar and was taken to hospital. Little Charlie followed the ambulance on his bicycle, leading the Major's dog on a long piece of string, and sat for hours in the waiting room until a Matron with a keen sense of smell ejected him.

Diagnosis on the Major was difficult. It was more a combination of small ailments than one big specific one. Old age for a start, with some nerve and tissue degeneration, poor circulation, a piece of shrapnel which was still moving about his body and occasionally blocking things, and a heart prone to stutter now and again.

He was sent home in a fortnight with strict instructions: plenty of rest, no excitement, no smoking and strictly no drinking until further notice.

It is probably uncharitable to say that this was the chance Mrs Hawkins had been waiting for. She now had her husband all to herself, away from the friends and habits she had so long disapproved of, and she kept him virtually a prisoner in his own home.

Charlie went round to see the Major once only. Mrs Hawkins's nose wrinkled with distaste when she opened the door. She allowed Charlie upstairs only on the understanding that he didn't stay too long. He stayed more than long enough. From his haversack he produced a bottle of scotch, the result of a collection by the public bar regulars. He and the Major swigged great gulps of it in tea cups and by the time Mrs Hawkins came up to investigate, they were both roaring drunk.

That did it. Out went Charlie, never to return. From then on none of the Major's cronies was allowed across the threshold. For six months the poor man saw nobody but his wife. Only one concession was made to Charlie. He was allowed to walk the Major's dog twice a day. There was no contact with the house.

The dog was tied to the gatepost for Charlie to pick up and Charlie tied it up there again on his return. After six months the Major was able to venture out, not too far at first, but gradually a reasonable distance until that distance stretched to the Tadchester Arms.

He walked into the public bar and it was as if he had never been away. He and Charlie moved straight into the mutual insults routine and Charlie demonstrated to the Major how much his dog had improved under the Sloper training course. Charlie had taught the dog to carry beer mats from one person to another. He sent one over to the Major. The Major wrote on it, 'Thanks for everything, you squalid little man,' and sent it back by return of dog. Charlie sent his reply on the mat. It said, simply, 'Piss orf'.

The two old enemies, the two best of old friends, were back in business . . .

15

Assorted Characters

Since the turn of the century, Tadchester had had its own prize silver band. Over the years its fortunes fluctuated, depending on how much the town council of the time was prepared to finance it, and on the ability and industry of the bandmaster who happened to be in control over any particular period.

It was certain that the band reached its peak just after World War Two under the influence of the bandmaster, Leighton Evans. It won competition after competition, and even played at the Albert Hall in London in a national competition.

Leighton was a Welshman from the valleys who had been invalided out of the coal-mines with silicosis. He put all his Welsh fervour into his love of music and the Tadchester silver band was his pride and joy. With the baton in his hand he was an absolute tyrant. He spared nobody at practice. The bandsmen (and particularly the town's junior band) were terrified of him. But he cajoled, threatened, encouraged and inspired them to musical heights far beyond their normal capabilities.

In addition to his musical capabilities, Leighton was the most accident prone man that I have ever met. At one time or other he had broken twenty-three bones in his body. Later he developed severe rheumatoid arthritis, which drastically limited his mobility, apart from causing a lot of pain and discomfort, and finally developed cataracts in both eyes.

He had tremendous courage and somehow survived all his

incredible medical conditions, was much more alive than most, highly intelligent, and a tremendous ally.

We developed a great friendship. We both had mining in common (I had had my two years down the mines as a Bevin Boy at the end of World War Two) and had a language of our own. When I visited him, we had a marvellous repartee. I would say, 'Bloody miners. Its all featherbeds down the pits nowadays.'

'Bloody doctors,' Leighton would reply. 'They have so much money now, they are having to bury it in tins in the garden.'

Mrs Evans would make us a cup of tea and we would sit talking – coal mines, socialism, the town council – and generally putting the world to rights. Leighton was an ardent socialist, very articulate about his beliefs, and a great fighter for social justice. He was also a good business man. He always knew of bargains, somewhere where you could get musical instruments for half price, a place in Wales where you could buy men's suits from the factory for a quarter of the market price. He was always bright, never depressed, and it was almost impossible to stop him talking.

His first medical condition was silicosis. It was not too bad, but prevented him from working underground, and made him very prone to chest infections.

Leighton's salary as bandmaster was not sufficient to maintain him, so he made up the deficit by doing a part-time job with one of the timber merchants who operated from Tadchester Quay.

His first accident there was when some timber fell on him, crushing both his feet.

After innumerable operations, he finished up by having to have both his ankles fused. This relieved some of the pain but meant he had two stiff, unbending ankles.

He then developed rheumatoid arthritis. His hands and fingers became twisted and he could no longer play musical instruments. His knees became swollen and fixed, to be followed shortly by the same condition affecting his hips, limiting his walking to a few shambling steps with a walking frame. This was in spite of all the modern drugs, including Cortisone, that were available.

'This won't do, Doctor,' said Leighton. 'I have to get walking again.'

I sent him to every specialist I thought might help him. There were various operations which gave some relief, but his fixed knees and hips seemed at an impasse.

Then a new orthopaedic surgeon was appointed to Winchcombe, with new techniques and appliances. At first Leighton was given metal hinges in his knees, then he had hip replacements on both sides. Before you could have imagined it possible, there was Leighton walking round the town with a stick, and driving his car to brass band concerts.

He had invested the compensation for both his silicosis and his leg injury and was able to live comfortably, if not extravagantly. He and his wife had a house in Stonehouse Street, on a steep road leading down to Tadchester pannier market. He had known days of extreme poverty in the depressions of the thirties, was penny wise, and was determined that his two children should have security. His daughter married a successful engineer. His son, Owen, as well as winning the national solo trumpet crown, passed his matriculation and got a good job with the Inland Revenue. In his later years, Leighton said proudly, 'I never thought, Doctor, that I would have two grandsons at a public school and two granddaughters at a private convent.'

'You always were a bloody capitalist at heart, Leighton,' I said.

His reply would not have been repeatable at chapel in Tonypandy.

* * *

I asked Leighton's advice about music education for Trevor and Paul. I would have liked them to have played an instrument. What did he suggest?

'Send them to me,' he said. 'You want to start them on the cornet. In a brass band you start playing tunes early, so you don't lose interest, and you do it with a lot of mates.'

'How old should they be when they start?' I asked.

'Eight years old,' said Leighton. 'Send them to me when Trevor is eight.'

Soon after Trevor's eighth birthday he and Paul, who was then five, would be met by Leighton from school and go back to his house for tea and for Trevor's instruction on the cornet. Before each lesson they had to have a traditional Welsh tea. On their first visit Mrs Evans, in as musical a Welsh voice as her husband, said, 'What would you boys like?'

'What is Owen having?' asked Trevor.

'Beans on toast,' said Mrs Evans.

'Beans on toast, please,' said Trevor. If Owen ate beans on toast, they were obviously a great aid to trumpet playing.

'What about you, Paul?' asked Mrs Evans.

As far as food went, Paul knew exactly what he wanted.

'Egg and chips, please, Mrs Evans.'

Whatever Paul's activities, then or since, egg and chips have been the fuel and inspiration.

This became their Friday evening nourishment. Every Friday for ten years Trevor and Paul would go to tea with the Evanses, Trevor to have beans on toast and Paul to have egg and chips, and Leighton would talk and instruct them both about music.

Trevor joined the youth band and eventually graduated from the cornet to the trumpet. The only time he doubted Leighton's wisdom was when, following his advice, he and a group of boys from the band spent forty-eight hours at an army camp to see whether they would like the idea of becoming army bandsmen. Trevor hated it. He loved his creature comforts and reveille at 0600 hours, with a cold shower and drill, was not his idea of musical fun.

Leighton made Trevor into a proficient trumpet player, good enough to fill in for local orchestras, and a tremendous asset to the jazz club when he went to university. And Trevor formed a great affection for him.

When Trevor went on holiday after we, the family, had moved away, it was always with Leighton that he went to stay.

When I last saw Leighton I broke the news that Trevor, who by now had two law degrees, had given it all up to go to drama school.

'I knew he would do something like that,' said Leighton. 'Six months after he had started his law school he said to me, "Leighton, there seems to be one law for the rich and one for the poor. I don't know if I like that".'

'Had you been indoctrinating him, Leighton?' I asked.

'No, boyo,' said Leighton. 'I taught him music. Somebody else taught him law . . .'

* * *

Leighton was still as bright as ever, with seven or eight more operations under his belt, the latest being for cataracts in both eyes. He still managed to get about with two elbow crutches, and was as full of vim, vigour and courage as anyone.

'Did I tell you about my latest accident?' he said.

'No,' I replied.

'Well,' he said, 'I was given a lift to the Institute, got out of the car, and fell down a bloody hole in the road. I couldn't attract anyone's attention until a motorist saw my sticks in the road and came looking to see what was wrong. I was real shaken up. He helped me up and I managed to walk into the Institute, but I couldn't make it home; somebody had to run me back.

'I was in bed for a fortnight. I could hardly move my leg, my chest and arm hurt, and the wife had to lift me on to the potty.

'I was getting worse, and in the end I had to send for the doctor. He got me straight into hospital and they x-rayed me: broken pelvis, three broken ribs and a broken arm. No wonder I wasn't walking properly.

'I was in hospital for three months, came home, and then a week later I started coughing. Coughed up about two pints of blood.

'Back into hospital, blood transfusions and antibiotics. Now, thank God, I'm back out on my feet again. They said it was my old silicosis.'

He continued, 'It was funny in hospital the last time. This young lad of a doctor came to examine me and said, "What is wrong with you, Mr. Evans?"

'Not a lot,' I said. 'You will find my ankles are fixed solid, I have got metal hinges instead of knees, both my hips have been replaced and I have got silicosis. Now it hurts down below, my arm and chest hurt and I'm coughing up blood.'

The young lad said, "We shouldn't keep you in the ward. I think we'd better take you straight to the museum".'

Leighton was irrepressible. He survived all his major medical catastrophes by sheer spirit and determination. Half of what he had had would have killed most people. He brought the gift of music to Tadchester and instilled the love of music in my boys. Leighton would always battle on until he dropped, and dropping was only a transient time until he picked himself up again. I was proud to have him as a friend.

*   *   *

Tadchester was too small for Harry Walters, but he made little effort to get out of the place, perhaps because as a youth pleasurable things came too easy. Strong, athletic and good looking, he concentrated at school on girls instead of exams. Though he had a good brain, he ended his schooldays with nothing to show for it.

Called up for National Service he enlisted in the Grenadier Guards, hoping to see action in Korea or in one of the minor wars Britain was engaged in at the time. His battalion, however, stayed at home.

Life in the Guards was certainly no rest cure. But though he saw plenty of action with au pair girls in darkest Chelsea and once led his squad in a mock night attack on Salisbury Plain, ambushing a flock of sheep instead of the Scots Guards, he did not get the testing his restless mind and tough physique craved for.

He returned to Tadchester after his service even more restless. He had tasted London life, and Tadchester High Street was not exactly the King's Road. After two or three years of drinking, fighting and wenching he married, got a steady job and settled down. At least he settled down as far as someone like Harry Walters could.

Two years after his settling down I was called out to treat him twice in the same evening. The karate craze had come to Tadchester and Harry was one of the first to enrol in the club. At a party at his home one night, well-oiled, he insisted on demonstrating how to break a plank in half with one blow.

Either he hadn't quite mastered the art, or the plank was thicker than he bargained for, and he broke his hand very badly.

Harry's wife phoned me. After one look at his hand I drove him down to Tadchester Hospital. He was supported on the back seat by one of his mates so that he wouldn't fall over and do any more damage.

I had to call out my surgical colleague, Henry Johnson, to come and put the hand straight. We could not give Harry a general anaesthetic because of the amount of booze he had on board. Using local anaesthetics, Henry had to deaden the nerves that supplied the hand before putting things straight. He completed the setting job by enclosing the lower arm in plaster of paris.

Harry lived not too far from me so I drove him back home, where his anxious wife took over and steered him through the carousing guests upstairs to bed. Half an hour later Harry's wife phoned me again. She'd got him in his pyjamas, supporting the plaster with a sling, and put him to bed. The party was still going strong downstairs, however, and Harry didn't want to miss any fun. Over he rolled, fell out of bed and dislocated his shoulder.

Concussion was the next thing I treated him for. He came home from work one summer evening when the neighbourhood children – by now he had two young boys of his own – were playing Batman and charging about in capes and improvised batmobiles.

'BATMAN!' he yelled, spreading out his jacket, and jumped

clear over a five foot fence in some form of western roll. He
landed on his head and was just coming round when I arrived.

The children thought it was marvellous fun. 'That was great
Dad, do it again,' his eldest boy was saying. 'Yes, Uncle Harry,'
chanted the neighbours' children. 'Please – just once.' His reply
was not one of those recommended by Dr Spock.

Harry's right hand came in for a lot of damage one way or
another. One of his boys was once badly knocked about by a big
boy at school.

'There's only one way to settle this,' Harry said to his son.
'No matter how big he is, hit him first – like this'. So saying, he
spun round and aimed a fearsome blow at the living room door.
His fist went straight through the panel. It took me some time to
get the splinters out and strap up the dislocated fingers and torn
ligaments.

Fire drill was next. There had been a kitchen fire along the
road. Thankfully nobody was hurt, but Harry decided to give
his boys an object lesson on how to escape from a burning
house.

'Say you are standing at the top of stairs like this,' he said, watched from below by the wide-eyed boys who knew their father had the answer to everything. 'The hall is clear, but the whole staircase is alight. What do you do?'

One of the lads volunteered, 'Climb out through the back window.'

'Rubbish! No time for messing about. What you do is this.'

With a 'Hup!' he vaulted over the banister rail at the top of the stairs and plunged down into the hallway below. Or he would have plunged if his hand had not slipped on the banister. It jammed between two of the rails, pulled him up sickeningly short, and left him dangling in mid-air.

'It's a wonder your hand is still on the end of your arm,' I said as I strapped up, splinted and bound it. 'You're at an age now where you should be learning a bit more sense.'

'You're right, Doc,' he said. 'You're not wrong, you're dead right. From now on you are going to see a change. You are now looking at the new Harry Walters.'

The new Harry Walters turned out to be not all that much different from the old one. He came in one day looking harassed.

'I don't know, Doc,' he said. 'I think it's my nerves. Perhaps it's the quiet domestic life I'm leading. Perhaps it's family responsibilities. But I keep getting butterflies in my stomach, my hands tremble, I wake up in the middle of the night worrying about my job, the bank manager, the mortgage, the electricity bills and all that sort of stuff. And I get up in the morning absolutely whacked.'

I gave him a course of mild sedatives and warned him, 'Go easy on the booze. These pills and draught bitter don't mix.'

'Sure, Doc. I've been cutting down lately.'

During the next fortnight I kept hearing disturbing stories about Harry's behaviour. He was barred from three pubs in the town after fights. One evening coming home from work in his car he hit one of his brick gateposts and demolished it. A week later he demolished the other. Then he announced to his family that he was going off into the moors above Tadchester to go back to nature and live off the land for a while.

Off he went in his car singing *Born Free* at the top of his voice. He was back shortly after nightfall complaining that there was nowhere on the moors where he could plug in his electric blanket.

I was mulling over his antics during a lull in the evening surgery and thinking that perhaps I would call on him, when I was saved the trouble. The next patient was Harry himself. A little glassy-eyed and not in a good mood.

'Here, Doc,' he said, banging the plastic pill container on my desk. 'You can have the rest of these bloody things back. I've not been right since I started them. In fact I reckon you have given me the wrong prescription.'

'Now then, Harry,' I said. 'Simmer down. I've heard of one or two of your little adventures lately, and obviously something is not agreeing with you.'

'Too right. It's those bloody pills.'

'Remember that I warned you about drinking, and you said you were cutting it down.'

'Correct, but you can't rush these things. I've been doing it gradually.'

'How much do you drink a day?'

'Not a lot. Perhaps three or four pints at lunch time, and at night perhaps seven or eight.'

'And then you worry about the bank manager, the mortgage, and the electricity bills?'

'Yes. Ah . . . er . . . Well I've got to have some relaxation.'

'I'll keep these pills, Harry,' I said, 'and won't prescribe any more. You stick to your sedatives, and until you really cut down on them, I'll stick to mine.'

During the five minute chat which followed, I suggested tactfully that Harry might consider joining Alcoholics Anonymous. He seemed to consider this an excellent idea, and went out whistling.

It's strange what curious blind spots people can have: odd bits missing from the jigsaw of knowledge which most of us have in our day-to-day information banks.

I met Harry in the street a fortnight later. He came out of the Tadchester Arms.

'How's it going?' I asked. 'Did you do anything about my suggestion?'

'Oh, yes,' he said. 'But they wanted me to stop drinking. What kind of an outfit is that?'

'What kind did you think it was?' I asked.

'What its name suggested. Alcoholics Anonymous. A private drinking club where you didn't have to give your name.'

In spite of his eccentricities, or perhaps because of them, Harry was a very likeable character. Even the neighbours he upset or punched could not stay out of friends for long. He went his merry, boozy, erratic way of life, living up to his motto of 'Sod 'em all' until his boys were well into their teens. And then he changed.

Part of it might have been switching his job. He went to work one morning to be greeted by some petty quibble from his boss.

'That's it!' he exploded. 'You can stick your job!' and jammed a wastepaper basket over the boss's head.

He went from there to the labour exchange, and by some fantastic stroke of fate walked straight into another job, out of doors, which suited him right down to the ground. By this time one of his boys was working, and his wife was free to take a job of her own, so money was not a problem.

Another reason for the change might have been an impromptu karate match between him and his eldest son, now a strapping seventeen-year-old. Harry misplaced a kick which caught the lad in a very sensitive spot, and to a seventeen-year-old a very precious one. The lad lashed out in pain and temper and laid his father unconscious on the hearth rug. Perhaps Harry then realised that nobody can remain invincible for ever.

The final reason for the change, or perhaps a result of it, was his sudden passion for gardening. For years he had neglected the garden, paying the boys a few shillings for pushing the mower around once or twice a year. Then one day he bought himself a complete kit of gardening tools and started digging furiously. Within a week the whole garden was turned into a vegetable patch, dug, manured, hoed, raked – the soil was rich and friable, so there was no waiting for frost to break it down – and planted with all kinds of seeds. All his spare time from then on was spent in the garden. The pubs saw him only occasionally at weekends, and then he usually turned up in his gardening clothes, making time just for a couple of quick ones.

'My, my,' I said one day as I admired the profusion of healthy, tidy and edible greenery, 'you have made a grand job of the garden.'

'Yes,' he said with a wry grin. 'Makes you spit, doesn't it? But even Peter Pan had to come down to earth some time.'

* * *

Two of my patients had each lost a leg – one in a riding accident, and one by an anti-personnel mine during the war. Each had adjusted to his handicap in a totally different way. Though they did not know it, they were neighbours. And the adjustments they had made were to lead them into a bizarre confrontation.

Edward Murdock was a successful chartered accountant, with a large and flourishing practice. He lived in a mock Tudor house at the top of the great sweep of ground which rose up the hill from the banks of the Tad.

Always an active, vigorous man, his passion was riding. He rode to hounds, rode in local point-to-point races and show-jumping events. Almost every spare minute he spent in the saddle. One day, as he was hacking home from a hunt, a lorry rounded a corner on the wrong side of the road and spooked the horse. The horse shied and threw Murdock under the wheels. His leg had to be amputated from the thigh, and his riding days were over.

Eventually he took up shooting. His grounds were large enough, even though strictly speaking he might be breaking the law. There was enough small wild life around – crows, pigeons, squirrels, rabbits, even the occasional stray deer – to provide him with targets.

From then on nothing on his land was safe. Even one or two

of the local cats finished up dead by mistake. And when the natural game ran short, he started raising pheasants and partridges, releasing them when they were grown, and blasting the daylights out of them.

One far corner of Edward's land adjoined the back garden of a local painter and sculptor, Leslie Barnes. The two pieces of land, so dissimilar in size, were separated by a natural copse. Indeed, so well separated were the two that the owners had no real idea who was on the other side. Murdock knew that someone with a relatively small garden lived there. Leslie knew that somebody with pots of money and land to match, lived on the other side of what he regarded as 'his' copse.

Leslie was an animal sculptor and painter of extreme skill and sensitivity, and he used as his models the many animals and birds which used his garden as a sanctuary. Leslie would harm no living thing, and despised anybody who did, especially if they did it for sport.

He had not always been so caring and gentle. In his youth, before the war, shooting had been his one passion. All his spare time had been spent with a gun in his hand and he would shoot anything that moved.

He was quite happy in the army. It was but a small step from shooting animals to shooting people, and the ethics of it never bothered him.

One day, towards the end of the war in Europe, he found himself in Austria. The German troops had retreated, there was no action for miles, so he took himself off with his service rifle into a forest which abounded with deer.

He was a natural hunter, and it was not long before a stag was kicking on the ground about fifty yards away. Leslie started towards it to give it the *coup de grâce*. Halfway across the open ground there was an explosion and he was lying there, one leg gone and the other badly shattered.

The next ten minutes or so were an eerie experience. He lay there apparently doomed to bleed to death, facing a stag which was also bleeding to death. He had failed, he thought, as a hunter. He had not killed the stag outright. It was still kicking, and in pain. So he dragged himself painfully on his stomach, took careful aim, and put the stag out of its misery. Then he turned over, bound a handkerchief tightly round the stump of his leg, and started to drag himself out of the wood.

Luckily for him a patrol heard the shot and came into the wood to investigate. Leslie's life was saved. But his leg was not.

Discharged from the army with a disability pension and a tin leg, he tackled his problems completely differently from Edward Murdock. He had known real pain for the first time in his life, realised it was the kind that he had been inflicting for years on living creatures, and decided to cause no more pain to anything.

He came to Tadchester, bought the small cottage by the Tad with a garden which ran up to the copse, and started on the animal painting and sculpting by which he eventually was to earn a living and some small fame.

Before long his garden had become a miniature wildlife sanctuary. Birds of all kinds, squirrels, rabbits, badgers, deer, and the occasional fox used to appear and eat the food that he left out for them. If he appeared, the creatures were in no hurry to move away: they seemed to sense that he meant them no harm.

One particular fox he grew very fond of, and it grew fond of him. Though it would not actually eat out of his hand, it came close enough for him to throw it scraps of meat. It would sit there and eat while Leslie watched.

After its morning meal one day the fox slipped back into the copse. Five minutes later there was the sound of a shot from Murdock's land, and the fox re-emerged in Leslie's garden with half its side blown away by shotgun pellets.

Leslie sank onto his knees, the metal joint in his leg squeaking. The fox put its head on his lap, as though it were a faithful housedog, and died.

There was a crashing about in the copse and Murdock appeared at the boundary.

'I say! You there!' he shouted.

In his sculptor's smock Leslie looked the archetypal peasant.

Murdock *was* trying to re-assert himself so that would explain, if not excuse, his apparent rudeness.

'You seen anything of a fox?'

Leslie lifted the bloodied form from his knee.

'This it?'

'Ah, yes. Mine, I think.'

Murdock climbed stiffly over the boundary fence (by now he too had been fitted with an artificial leg) and strode towards Leslie who, with the aid of his walking stick, was struggling upright.

It was the walking stick that laid Murdock unconscious across the fox, and which also did considerable damage to Murdock's ribs as he lay there. Leslie took up Murdock's gun, broke the expensive thing in half against a tree. Then he phoned the police.

I treated Murdock at his home. He was raving and threatening to press all sorts of charges. I explained about Leslie's disability and he calmed down.

Leslie visited him the next day, stayed for a long talk, and thereafter the two got on reasonably well. They never became close friends but they were sensible enough to live and let live, and they were helped by the realisation that someone else had the same disability.

'What frightened me,' said Leslie when he came into the surgery one day for treatment for chafing on his stump, 'was my reaction after I had laid Murdock out. There was a cartridge still left in that gun and my finger had actually taken up the slack on the trigger before I remembered the deer in the woods all that time ago. Just goes to show how thin the line is between . . .'

'Between?'

'St Francis of Assisi and Attila the bloody Hun,' he said. 'See you, Doc. Be good.'

16

Round in Circles

I had to go to London to attend a two-day postgraduate course at a chest hospital. These courses always caused me some disquiet. Obviously it was important to keep up with the latest trends of medicine but usually, in learning the new advances, I was shown the deficiencies and dangers of the old techniques and apparatus that I was using.

This applied particularly to my hospital work. I would learn that only the new super deluxe electrocardiogram gave proper recordings, and the particular machine I was using at the time was not only no good, but dangerous.

Having absorbed all the new and valuable information I would then have to go back to Tadchester and use my old equipment: apparatus that had never let me down and which, before the course, I would have trusted with my life. Now I used it with the worry that not only was it no good, it was lethal. I knew also that I had no alternative but to go on using it: it would be at least ten years before the latest advances reached Tadchester.

Happily, medicine tends to go round in circles and by the time the new equipment and techniques had reached Tadchester, the circle had been almost completed. It was the new machine that was now held to be faulty and they were using something very like my old machine as the most wonderful and latest advance.

This cycle of thinking affected almost all areas of medicine. In later years in the National Health Service it was decided to shut all the small hospitals and build more large ones. So one by one all the cottage hospitals like Tadchester were closed down and huge structures catering for thousands of patients erected all over the country.

Just before, or just as, the last small hospital was shut down, some senior bureaucrats had a wonderful idea. These huge healing palaces that they'd built didn't work all that well for the patient who needed hospital care but didn't need too specialised treatment. Why not a community hospital so each community had its own? Where elderly patients and others not requiring major surgery or medical treatment could be looked after by the people of the community that they lived in? Where their general practitioners could keep a day to day eye on them? Where they wouldn't take up the more expensive beds in these bigger highly specialised hospitals? Cottage hospitals – what a splendid idea.

So as soon as they had closed all the cottage hospitals down they started building new cottage hospitals again. I am sure the bureaucrat who thought up the idea got knighted for his brilliant and original thought.

*   *   *

I had to spend two nights in London for the course at the chest hospital. Pam had a lot of home commitments and could not come with me, so I was to stay with my old friend Albert. We had both been Bevin Boys together at Dinnington Colliery in 1945–46. I had worked on the coal face but Albert had opted to be a pit pony driver – much the more hazardous of the two jobs. His strong, overfed and underworked pony used to give him the most hair raising time.

After leaving the mines, Albert had started up in a modest way as a jeweller in Birmingham. He had prospered and had moved to London to be closer to Hatton Garden. We had kept in touch, mainly at Christmas, but had seen each other only intermittently over the intervening years. It seemed a good opportunity to renew our acquaintance and I wrote to ask if he could put me up for one night. He and his wife replied with the most welcoming invitation.

I didn't realise how successful Albert had been until I approached his house in one of the more expensive parts of Hampstead. I turned into a gravel drive in this most expensive looking area and drove up to a large Georgian house. As I drove up I could hear the baying of dogs . . . and one of my big fears had always been of large dogs.

Albert and Mary came to the door to greet me. My first question was, 'You've got some dogs?'

'Yes. We'll let them out in a minute. They won't bother you – just stand still until they get used to you.'

My heart sank.

'Now!' shouted Albert. A manservant opened a door, and out bounded two snarling Alsatians. They came up to me, looked me over and sniffed me up and down. After what seemed like hours they left me alone and went about their business.

'It's all right. You can move now,' said Mary. 'They just like to get to know you. Jenny, the small one,' – Jenny looked huge to me – 'is my favourite, and Rover, the big one, is Albert's. We have so many diamonds in the house that we have to have some protection.'

During my stay I was very wary of these dogs. The fact that the dogs knew I was terrified of them didn't help. Once in an unguarded moment, when I walked in part of the house unaccompanied by Albert or Mary, the dog sitting nearest let a low rumbling noise from its throat. It sounded like the lowest note of an organ. I retreated slowly – and backwards.

'They're marvellous dogs,' said Mary that evening after dinner. 'We've had so many robberies here that we just have to have some form of security. Thieves broke in up the road and held the houseowners at gunpoint. They tortured the dog until they told them where the valuables were, and then killed it. But theirs was a little dog – I can't imagine a burglar subduing these two, even with a machine gun.'

The evening and the meal they gave me were delightful. Albert and Mary were really good and old friends – Albert was Trevor's godfather – and he and I had a marvellous evening reminiscing about our days down the mines.

It so often happens that one's best friends live at a distance, and one never seems able to find time to get to see them. There just aren't enough days in the year.

After a long evening full of reminiscences, brandy and cigars, we went to bed. The two dogs slept in huge baskets outside Albert and Mary's room. We had wined and dined well and I went to bed in a happy, relaxed state and slept soundly.

I was awakened in the early hours by my body telling me it wanted to get rid of the excess fluid I had taken in during the evening.

I opened the door to go to the bathroom. As I did so, two low pitched growls emitted from the baskets outside Albert and Mary's door. As I stepped closer both these growls increased in volume and I imagined the huge snarling jaws in the darkness of the corridor.

I went back to bed, thinking I would just have to hang on somehow until morning. I stuck it for another hour and realised nature was going to win this battle. I mustn't be foolish about two dogs, I told myself: they'd been quite friendly. I opened the door boldly and took two steps down towards the bathroom. Immediately both dogs leapt snarling out of their baskets. I ran back into the bedroom and shut the door.

I was bursting. I had to choose between having a ruptured bladder or my throat torn out by the dogs. I was in total despair . . . until I looked in the corner of the room and saw the sink with the two shiny taps. I walked across, turned on one of the taps loudly to drown any other noise, and in a few minutes had relieved the situation. There was now no need to face the hazards of a journey to the bathroom.

I didn't tell Albert and Mary of my adventures during the night. Friendship can only be stretched so far, and the beautiful furnishings and fittings of the house didn't quite fit in with my communion with the bedroom sink.

I was spending the next night in a London hotel with toilet and bathroom en suite, so even if there had been a wolf pack roaming the corridors, I wouldn't have any problems getting to the toilet.

*　　*　　*

On the second day of the postgraduate course we were introduced to a machine, then a new invention, that measured one's breathing capacity. By blowing into this machine you could tell how efficient your personal breathing apparatus was. Called a peak flow meter, the machine was designed for assessing the progress of people with chronic chest disease.

The bearded intellectual professor who introduced the machine explained that it gave the answers to all questions on breathing, and stressed how important it was to disregard the patients' views on how they felt at any particular time. This was a great surprise to me. Certainly a new method of approach.

The professor said the patient might have taken a preparation for his breathing that made him feel better, but the peak flow meter could show in fact that his breathing was worse. On the other hand, he said, the patient might take a preparation for his breathing that made him feel worse, and the peak flow meter could show that he was in actual fact better. So one should disregard the patient's opinion and rely purely on this machine.

I envisaged a situation where I could be with a patient and not have one of these machines handy, and neither I nor the patient would be able to tell whether he was better or not.

My next-door neighbour at the lecture, an old rugby colleague – at postgraduate courses one always bumped into several old mates – whispered, 'I see. You're better when you feel worse and worse when you feel better. Why didn't I think of it before . . .'

Many years later I attended a course at the same chest hospital. There was a new generation of professors and lecturers, whose wrinkled brows and balding foreheads showed how intellectual they were. They thought that they would tell us general practitioners about this wonderful new discovery they had made.

'We have found,' said their spokesman, 'through our studies of patients with chest diseases over the years – and it is very important for all you chaps to remember this – that what the patient says is important. If a patient says that he is feeling better, then he probably is. By the same rule, if your patient says he is feeling worse, then it is quite probable that he is worse.'

I was sorry that my old rugby colleague who had sat next to me at the original lecture wasn't there for some comment.

Thinking had gone full circle in yet another branch of medicine. How profound, how intelligent, how learned were our tutors, and what a gem of wisdom I could take back to Tadchester with me. Let's get it right, now: if a patient said he felt worse, he was probably right, and if he said that he felt better, there was a good chance that he was improving. What an advance in medicine! And as yet nobody has produced another machine to disprove it . . .

*   *   *

It was strange being in London again after so many years. Having forty-eight hours there made me realise how much I appreciated living in Tadchester, being part of a well-defined community and having a part to play in that community. London was so impersonal and seemed to have changed a great deal since the days when I had been a student there. It was noisier, there seemed to be more cars, people appeared less polite, and of course everything was much more expensive.

I took my cases from the hotel to the hospital for the last day of my course so that I could get away, immediately after the last lecture, on the first available train to Tadchester.

I caught a taxi from the hospital to the station. I was cross-questioned by the taxi driver.

'You a doctor, Guv?' he asked.

'Yes,' I replied, expecting to be asked to make a diagnosis for some obscure condition on the spot. Instead, I got the taxi driver's life history.

He'd been driving a cab for forty-two years. 'In fact,' he said, 'I'm the only dead cab driver still driving.' He claimed he was the only man in England walking around with his own death certificate in his pocket.

'It was like this, Guv,' he said. 'My mother had a hard time with me when I was being born. When I was pulled out eventually I didn't breathe, so they left me on one side. The doctor had to attend to mother. Then he had another look at me and said, "He's not going to do anything," and wrote out a death certificate on the spot.

'One of the neighbours wouldn't have it, and kept dipping me in and out of tubs of hot and cold water. Eventually she got me breathing. I was a sickly baby at first but grew up to be a perfectly healthy lad, played games and was keen on athletics.

'It was only when I went up for army service during the war they told me that I'd only got one lung. This was why I was so sickly at birth. One of me lungs hadn't opened, but me other lung grew to fill the whole of me chest. If they hadn't told me, I'd never have known. Anyway they wouldn't let me in the army, so I had to spend the war driving around in the blitz.

Probably much more dangerous than going to the front.'

'Have you ever thought of telling the Income Tax authorities you are not alive?' I asked him.

'Yes, Guv. I did once, and they said if I was dead I couldn't have a licence for me taxi. They win every time.'

We pulled up at Paddington Station. I got out and looked up at the departure board. It was somehow reassuring to see the notice that a train was due to depart for Taunton, Winchcombe and all stations to Tadchester and Dratchet.

I was on my way home. There was somewhere I belonged.

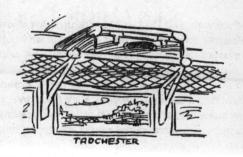

TADCHESTER

17

Moving House

Trevor was eight and Paul was coming up to five. No other child had appeared on the horizon and we felt that we would settle for the two boys as a family, although we would have dearly loved a girl.

Pam's parents, too, would have loved a granddaughter. Through Pam's brother, Thomas, they had three grandsons: our two made five, and they felt a girl would just make up the complement. But there was no sign of any impending new arrival.

As the boys grew bigger we were beginning to burst out of the seams of Herbert Barlow's flat. We looked round for a suitable house to buy. There was one in Altriston that we'd set our hearts on and got as far as putting a deposit down. We thought all was settled when the old lady from whom we were buying suddenly upped the price by several hundred pounds. This put it way beyond our reach. We had very bitter thoughts about the old girl, and started again from scratch. There didn't seem to be anything that we could afford within a reasonable distance. Then Kevin came to the rescue by offering a plot of ground by the river's edge, half way between Sanford-on-Sea and Tadchester.

This was almost too good to be true. His firm were selling off part of a larger estate. Not only did this threequarters of an acre have a marvellous view of the estuary, it was also full of different types of pine trees, part of a much larger garden and estate. The late owners, over several generations, had collected the most beautiful assortment of trees from all over the world. The new owner who was selling off part of the land was very particular to whom he sold: happily a doctor was to his taste and we were offered the ground very cheaply.

We had not ever thought of building and I had no idea how to begin, though we would obviously have to knock one or two of these beautiful trees down to get a house in at all. The land was on a steep gradient and I began to wonder whether it was possible. I also doubted whether I could afford architects' fees to survey and plan a house for us on this land.

Through Eric we managed to get the architect from the town and country planning office who'd do a bit of surveying and planning for people in his own time at a very much reduced rate paid in cash. Thumbing through a magazine we saw the plan of a house on a hill. We liked the look of it and our architect adapted it for us. He couldn't supervise the building, but we'd got the best quote from a builder patient whom I knew would be meticulous in his craftsmanship.

It was so exciting watching the house grow. First of all a bulldozer found a path through the trees, and only had to knock one or two down. Then it flattened a plateau that would not only enable us to build a house on it but would allow for an area in front where cars could turn, and which looked straight down over the estuary.

We turned the original house plan upside down so that our dining room and lounge and kitchen were upstairs, looking out over the estuary, and we went downstairs to sleep.

The house wasn't very big because we hadn't much money. It was terrifying to see a wheelbarrow almost filling a room that was going to be a bedroom.

Herbert was very sad to see us leave the flat, but had managed to let it to some retired theatre people who would be just his cup of tea.

At last the day came for us to move. Most of the stuff we moved in a van from Eric's shop. Kevin's father produced a

larger van to take our bigger furniture, and we did all the moving ourselves.

We loved our new house. It was really a house to be retired in. Through my lounge window I could watch the tide ebb and flow along the estuary. I could see the fishermen row up and shoot their nets in the river below the house. I could watch the wild birds and see heron standing on the bank fishing. Unfortunately I still had to work hard and didn't have enough time to stand and stare, but I never ever tired of the view.

I started to cultivate part of the garden. It was wild and full of thorn bushes where there weren't trees growing. Roy, Kevin's brother who worked for Somerset farmers, brought along the latest rotovators and cultivators and beat up the ground for me so that I would have a good start.

I bought a small dinghy that we moored down at the bottom of the garden. Unfortunately when the tide was out there was almost a quarter of a mile of estuary mud to walk across to reach the actual river.

We went up river for picnics and down river for fishing. It was three miles down the river to the mouth of the estuary. We were very enthusiastic at first but having once or twice lost our wellingtons in the mud, we only went out when the tide was right and the weather was right. The times when both these things were right and I was off duty and I wasn't wanting to do anything else, got fewer and fewer. But the thought of having a boat there if we wanted to use it was a tremendous boon.

We bought a little Cairn terrier, Susie. Trevor and Paul and Susie were in their seventh heaven in this new house. Racing up and down the river bank, fishing, following rabbits. There was something to do from dawn till dusk.

The only thing that had marred the move was that, just after we moved in, Pam's mother became unwell. After a lot of persuading she went into hospital to have some investigations. She had an operation and it was found that she had a widespread malignant disease. There was some chance that she might recover, but it was a very small chance.

Pam took the news of her mother's ill-health badly and started being unwell herself. I thought that this was probably in sympathy with her mother, but then I realised that she was ill in her own right – in fact she was pregnant again.

Pam took the news of both her mother's illness and the pregnancy very badly. She was terribly upset. Her mother was such a courageous person, always full of vim and vigour, adored and loved by her grandchildren, and had a special language with which she could talk with them. Trevor in particular played games with her for hours on end.

Pam realised that she was going to be occupied with her pregnancy during these last months of her mother's life when she would have liked to be able to devote all her time to her.

We had built the house for a family of four. We'd only been in for four months when we were having to knock down walls and rearrange things because we had to have a nursery for the baby which we hadn't anticipated.

As Pam's pregnancy progressed so did the general health of Bill, her mother, deteriorate. We were very lucky with our friends. Margaret Buck in particular took Pam and Bill as much as she could under her wing and did what she could for both of them. Bill got steadily worse and was admitted to hospital in the last month of Pam's pregnancy.

It was thought that she would be well enough to be allowed out of hospital for Christmas and Margaret Buck invited us all to stay with her. It was an awful Christmas. Everybody tried to be cheerful, but it was so terribly depressing seeing such a brave spirit as Bill going so painfully downhill. Gerry, her husband, could hardly hide his grief and there was no way we could console him. Pam, now so near the birth, was so depressed that her beloved mother was obviously going to leave her soon.

I do not know how we would have coped without Margaret Buck who looked after us all and remained cheerful throughout. She had lost her own husband some years before and appreciated what we were all going through.

We had to get Bill back to hospital as soon as Christmas was over. We were able to get a side ward for her in Tadchester Hospital where we knew we'd be able to keep her comfortable over the last few days of her life. Pam who had been in poorer health during this pregnancy than with either Paul or Trevor, was at the lowest I'd ever known her.

I visited Bill in hospital two or three times a day, and she was obviously deteriorating fast. I called in to see her one Saturday, obviously near her last. Pam wasn't certain whether she was in labour or not, but was too unwell to come up to the hospital. Bill took my hand.

'Never mind, Bob,' she said. 'Take care of Pam. I'm sorry I won't be alive to see the little girl.'

These were the last words she said to anybody. She died peacefully that night.

In the midst of all the worry and trauma of fixing up a funeral and making all sorts of other arrangements, Pam went into labour and was sent into Winchcombe Hospital. Her other labours had been quick but this one was prolonged and she was making heavy weather of it. She was still in labour on the Wednesday morning of Bill's funeral. I couldn't not go to the funeral. I knew Pam would want me there, and there was nothing I could do at the hospital. The staff wouldn't want me near the place.

I went with Gerry to the funeral and sat next to him, trying to comfort him as best I could. Poor Gerry: his wife was being buried and his only daughter was in hospital having a difficult labour. Life for him seemed full of bitterness and pain. He and Bill had been happily married for over forty years and there just didn't seem much to look forward to.

Towards the end of the funeral service I heard footsteps at the back of the church. I half turned round and saw Henry Johnson, my partner, creeping up the aisle of the church. He sidled along the pew behind me, reached forward between Gerry and myself and whispered in a loud voice (poor old Henry was incapable of speaking softly) 'All's well. It's a little girl, and Pam's all right.'

I saw Gerry's features brighten and it was as if a cloud had been lifted from above my own head.

Life was going to be different from now on.

Postscript

There is the fable of the old man sitting outside a town, being approached by a stranger.

'What are they like in this town?' asked the stranger.

'What were they like in your last town?' replied the old man.

'They were delightful people. I was very happy there. They were kind, generous and would always help you in trouble.'

'You will find them very much like that in this town.'

The old man was approached by another stranger.

'What are the people like in this town?' asked the second stranger.

'What were they like in your last town?' replied the old man.

'It was an awful place. They were mean, unkind and nobody would ever help anybody.'

'I am afraid you will find it very much the same here,' said the old man.

If it should be your lot to ever visit Tadchester, this is how you will find us.